COPY RIGHTS RESERVED 2020
TAMOH ART PUBLISHING

HOW TO PRAY
THE FIVE DAILY PRAYERS
IN ISLAM
FOR KIDS

278 Pages and 8x10 in

This book belongs to :

....

....

....

The Content of this book:

Page n°003: Salat Al- Fajr……………………………….

Page n°037: Salat Adduher……………………………..

Page n°097: Salat Al-Aaser………………………………

Page n°157: Salat Al-Maghreb………………………….

Page n°204: Salat Al-Aishaa……………………………..

Page n°265: Ablution in Islam…………………………..

HOW TO PRAY SALAT AL-FAJR

Number of Rakaahs:
Two Rakaahs.

Recitation of the Quran:
- **Boys**: Recite aloud.
- **Girls**: Recite silently

Time:
Dawn, before sunrise

So, let's start.

بإسم الله الرحمان الرحيم
« bismi llaahi rrahmaani rrahiime »
In the name of Allah, Most Gracious, Most Merciful.

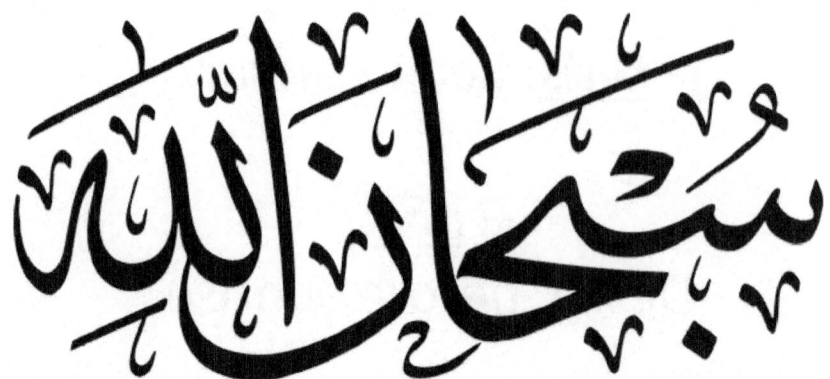

This is the illustration of the first « RAKAAH »

First, stand up, your face towards QIBLA, MECCA

Then, always start with « bismillaah »: in the name of Allah.

You should have the intention to pray and then say:

الله أكبر الله أكبر

«Allaahou akbar, allaahou akbar.»

Allah is Great, Allah is Great

أشهد أن لا إلاه إلا الله

« ashehadou anna laa ilaaha illa llaah »

I bear witness that there is no god but Allah

وأشهد أن محمدا عبده و رسوله

« wa ashehadou anna mohammadane abdouhou wa rassoulouhou »

And I bear witness that Muhammad is His slave and Prophet

حي على الصلاة حي على الفلاح

« hayya alaa ssalaati, hayya halaa lfalaahi »

Come to prayer, come to success

قد قامت الصلاة

«qade qaamati ssalaatou»

Prayer has been established,

الله أكبر الله أكبر

«allaahou akbar , allaahou akbar. »

Allah is Great, Allah is Great

لا إلاه إلا الله

« laa ilaaha illa llaah »

there is no god but Allah.

5

Then, start your prayer of Al-Fajr by saying:

الله أكبر

« allaahou akbar »

Allah is Great

- Look at the following image -

Then, recite aloud surah Al-Fatiha:

بإسم الله الرحمان الرحيم
« bismillaahi rrahmaani rrahiime »
In the name of Allah, Most Gracious, Most Merciful.

الْحَمْدُ لِلَّهِ رَبِّ الْعَالَمِينَ
« alhamdou lillaahi rabbi al-aalamiina »
Praise be to Allah, the Cherisher and Sustainer of the worlds,

الرَّحْمَٰنِ الرَّحِيمِ
« arrahmaani rrahiime »
Most Gracious, Most Merciful,

مَالِكِ يَوْمِ الدِّينِ
« maaliki yawemi ddiine »
Master of the Day of Judgment.

إِيَّاكَ نَعْبُدُ وَإِيَّاكَ نَسْتَعِينُ
« iyyaaka na-aboudo wa iyyaaka nasta-aaiine »
Thee do we worship, and Thine aid we seek.

اهْدِنَا الصِّرَاطَ الْمُسْتَقِيمَ
« ihdina ssiraata almoustaqiime »
Show us the straight way,

»صِرَاطَ الَّذِينَ أَنْعَمْتَ عَلَيْهِمْ غَيْرِ الْمَغْضُوبِ عَلَيْهِمْ وَلَا الضَّالِّينَ. امين.
« siraata lladiina ane-aameta aalayehime, ghayri almaghdoubi aalayehime, wala ddaliine. Amiiiiine »
The way of those on whom Thou hast bestowed Thy Grace, those whose (portion) is not wrath, and who go not astray. Amine.

7

After finishing ALFATIHA, recite aloud any verse from the Quran: For example: Surah AL IKHLAS

بسم الله الرحمن الرحيم
« bismillaahi rrahmaani rrahiime »
In the Name of Allâh, the Most Beneficent, the Most Merciful.

قُلْ هُوَ اللَّهُ أَحَدٌ
« qoul houa llaahou ahade »
Say "Allâh is (the) One

اللَّهُ الصَّمَدُ
« allaahou ssamade »
The Self-Sufficient Master

لَمْ يَلِدْ وَلَمْ يُولَدْ
« lame yalide walame youlade »
"He begets not, nor was He begotten.

وَلَمْ يَكُنْ لَهُ كُفُوًا أَحَدٌ
« walame yakoune lahou koufou-ane ahade »
And there is none co-equal or comparable unto Him.

Then, say: :

الله أكبر

« allaahou akbar »

Allah is Great

And, do as in the following image:

Then, say three times :

"subhaana rabiyya al-aaddiime » :

سبحان ربي العظيم

Glory be to my God

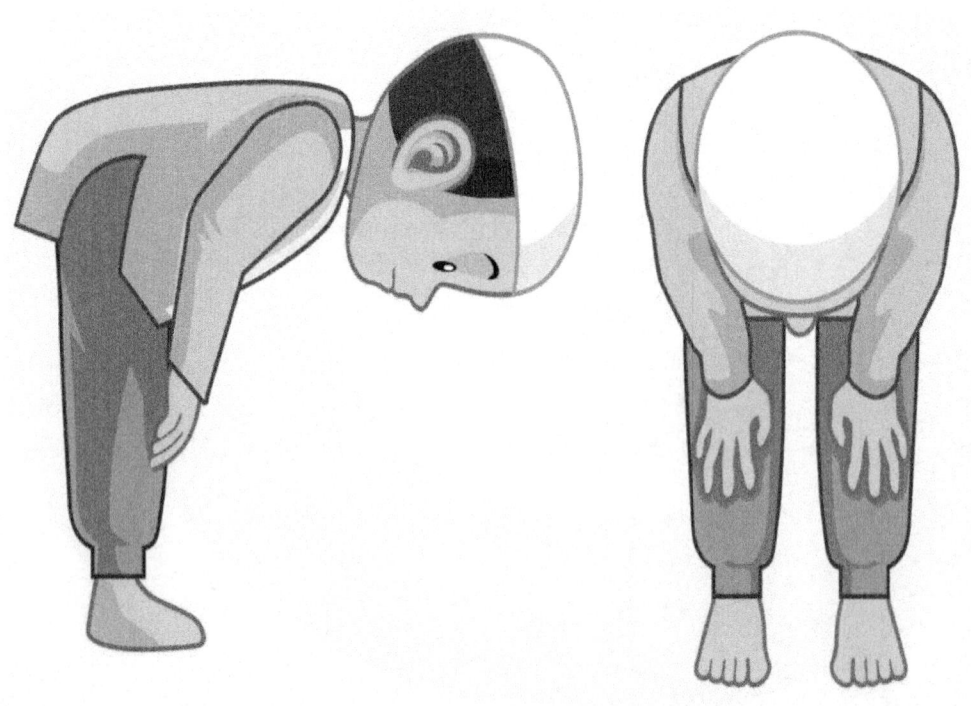

Then, standing upright again and saying:

"sami-aa llaahou liman hamidah" سمع الله لمن حمده

« Allah listens to those who praise Him »

« rabbanaa walaka lhamd » ربنا و لك الحمد

Praise be to our God

Then, say: :

الله أكبر

« allaahou akbar »

Allah is Great

While prostrating, you have to say 3 times :

"subhaana rabiyya al-aalaa"

سبحان ربي الأعلى

Glory to my God

Raising the head and saying:

"Allaahou akbar"

الله أكبر

Allah is Great

Then, say a request such as :

اللهم إغفر لي و إرحمني

« Allaahoumaa ighfir lii wa rhamnii »

My God, forgive me and have mercy on me

Then slowly bending down to prostrate and saying:

"Allaahou akbar"

الله أكبر

Allah is Great

Once again, while prostrating you have to say 3 times :

"subhaana rabiyya al-aalaa"

سبحان ربي الأعلى

Glory to my God

THE SECOND « RAKAAH »

This is the illustration of the second « RAKAAH »

Then, stand up again, your face towards the QIBLA, MECCA

Then, start your second RAKAAH by saying:

الله أكبر

« allaahou akbar »

Allah is Great

- Look at the following image -

Then, recite once again aloud surah Al-Fatiha:

بِسْمِ اللهِ الرحمان الرحيم
« bismillaahi rrahmaani rrahiime »
In the name of Allah, Most Gracious, Most Merciful.

الْحَمْدُ لِلَّهِ رَبِّ الْعَالَمِينَ
« alhamdou lillaahi rabbi al-aalamiine »
Praise be to Allah, the Cherisher and Sustainer of the worlds,

الرَّحْمَٰنِ الرَّحِيمِ
« arrahmaani rrahiime »
Most Gracious, Most Merciful,

مَالِكِ يَوْمِ الدِّينِ
« maaliki yawemi ddiine »
Master of the Day of Judgment.

إِيَّاكَ نَعْبُدُ وَإِيَّاكَ نَسْتَعِينُ
« iyyaaka na-aboudo wa iyyaaka nasta-aaiine »
Thee do we worship, and Thine aid we seek.

اهْدِنَا الصِّرَاطَ الْمُسْتَقِيمَ
« ihdina ssiraata almoustaqiime »
Show us the straight way,

»صِرَاطَ الَّذِينَ أَنْعَمْتَ عَلَيْهِمْ غَيْرِ الْمَغْضُوبِ عَلَيْهِمْ وَلَا الضَّالِّينَ. امين.
« siraata lladina ane-aameta aalayehime, ghayri almaghdoubi
 aalayehime, wala ddaliine. Amiiiiine »
The way of those on whom Thou hast bestowed Thy Grace, those whose (portion) is not wrath, and who go not astray. Amine.

After finishing ALFATIHA, recite aloud any verse from the Quran:
For example: سورة النصر *Surah An-Nasr*

بسم الله الرحمن الرحيم
« bismillaahi rrahmaani rrahiime »
In the Name of Allâh, the Most Beneficent, the Most Merciful.

إِذَا جَاءَ نَصْرُ اللَّهِ وَالْفَتْحُ
« idaa jaa a nasrou llaahi walfatehou »
When comes the Help of Allah, and Victory,

وَرَأَيْتَ النَّاسَ يَدْخُلُونَ فِي دِينِ اللَّهِ أَفْوَاجًا
« wa ra-ayeta nnaasa yadkhoulouna fii diini llaahi afwaajane »
And thou dost see the people enter Allah's Religion in crowds,

فَسَبِّحْ بِحَمْدِ رَبِّكَ وَاسْتَغْفِرْهُ إِنَّهُ كَانَ تَوَّابًا
« fasabbih bismi rabbika wa staghfirhou innahou kaana tawaabane »
Celebrate the praises of thy Lord, and pray for His Forgiveness: For He is Oft-Returning (in Grace and Mercy).

Then, say: :

الله أكبر

« allaahou akbar »

Allah is Great

And, do as in the following image:

Then, say three times :

"subhaana rabiyya al-aaddiime » :

سبحان ربي العظيم

Glory be to my God

Then, standing upright again and saying:

"sami-aa llaahou limane hamidah" سمع الله لمن حمده

« Allah listens to those who praise Him »

« rabbanaa walaka lhamd » ربنا و لك الحمد

Praise be to our God

Then, say: :

الله أكبر

« allaahou akbar »

Allah is Great

While prostrating, you have to say three times :

"subhaana rabiyya al-aalaa"

سبحان ربي الأعلى

Glory to my God

Raising the head and saying:

"Allaahou akbar"

الله أكبر

Allah is Great

Then, say a request such as :

اللهم إغفر لي و إرحمني

« Allaahoumma ighfir lii wa rhamenii »

My God, forgive me and have mercy on me

Then slowly bending down to prostrate and saying:

"Allaahou akbar"

الله أكبر

Allah is Great

Once again, while prostrating you have to say 3 times :

"subhaana rabiyya al-aalaa"

سبحان ربي الأعلى

Glory to my God

Raising the head and saying:

"Allaahou akbar"

الله أكبر

Allah is Great

Then, you sit on your knees to recite the tashahhud and Ibrahimya prayer, while moving your finger of your right hand:
(as written on the following page)

The Tashahhud and Ibrahimya prayer:

التحيات لله و الصلوات و الطيبات،
« attahiyaatou lillaah wa ssalawaatou wa ttayibaate »
All compliments, prayers and pure words are due to Allaah.

السلام عليك أيها النبي ، و رحمة الله و بركاته
« assalaamou aalayeka ayouha nnabii warahmatou llaahi wa barakaatouhou »
Peace be upon you, O Prophet, and the mercy of Allaah and His blessings.

السلام علينا و على عباد الله الصالحين،
« assalaamou aalayenaa wa aalaa aibaadi llaahi ssaalihiina »
Peace be upon us and upon the righteous slaves of Allaah.

أشهد أن لا إله إلا الله،
« ashehadou anna laa ilaaha illa llaah »
I bear witness that there is no god except Allaah

و أشهد أن محمدا عبده و رسوله.
« wa ashehadou anna mouhammadane aabedouhou wa rasoulouhou »
and I bear witness that Muhammad is His slave and Messenger.

اللهم صلي على محمد و على آل محمد
« allahoumma salli aalaa mouhammadine wa aalaa aali mouhammadine »
O Allaah, send prayers upon Muhammad and upon the family of Muhammad,

كما صليت على إبراهيم و على آل إبراهيم
« kamaa sallayeta aalaa ibrahiim wa aalaa aali ibrahiim »
as You sent prayers upon Ibraaheem and the family of Ibraaheem

وبارك على محمد و على آل محمد
« wa baarik aalaa mouhammadine wa aalaa aali mouhammadine »
O Allaah, bless Muhammad and the family of Muhammad

كما باركت على إبراهيم و على آل إبراهيم
« kamaa baarakta aalaa ibrahiim wa aalaa aali ibrahiim »
as You blessed Ibraaheem and the family of Ibraaheem,

في العالمين إنك حميد مجيد.
« fii l aalamiina innaka hamiidoune majiide »
You are indeed Worthy of Praise, Full of Glory.

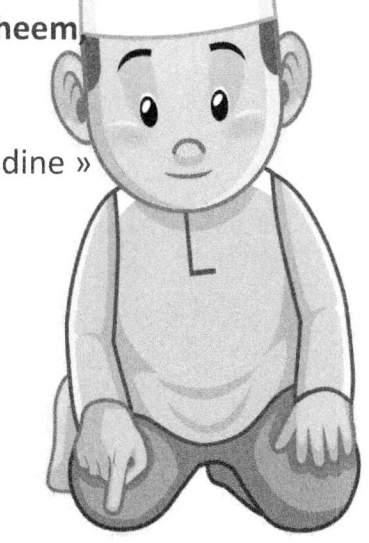

The termination of the prayers takes place as follows:

The head is turned to the right and you say:

"Assalaamou aalaykoum wa rahmatou llaahi ta-aalaa wa barakaatouh"

السلام عليكم و رحمة الله تعالى و بركاته

Peace, mercy and blessings of Almighty God

Then the head is turned to the left and you say:

"Assalaamou aalaykoum wa rahmatou llaahi ta-aalaa wa barakaatouh"

السلام عليكم و رحمة الله تعالى و بركاته

Peace, mercy and blessings of Almighty God

After finishing your prayer, you can say your request « Dua »

اللهم إني أسألك برحمتك التي وسعت كل شي أن تغفر لي

« allahoumma innii as-alouka birahmatika allatii
Wasi-aate koulla shaye-ine ane taghfira lii »

O Allaah, I ask you by your mercy which envelopes all things, that you forgive me.

HOW TO PRAY
SALAT ADDUHER

Number of Rakaahs:
Four Rakaahs.

Recitation of the Quran:
Both boys and girls have to recite silently.

Time:
Midday, after the sun passes its highest

So, let's start.

بإسم الله الرحمان الرحيم
« Bismi llaahi rrahmaani rrahiime »
In the name of Allah, Most Gracious, Most Merciful.

This is the illustration of the first « RAKAAH »

First, stand up, your face towards QIBLA, MECCA

Then, always start with « bismillaah »: in the name of Allah.

You should have the intention to pray and then say:

الله أكبر الله أكبر
«Allaahou akbar, allaahou akbar.»
Allah is Great, Allah is Great

أشهد أن لا إلاه إلا الله
« ashehadou anna laa ilaaha illa llaah »
I bear witness that there is no god but Allah

وأشهد أن محمدا عبده و رسوله
« wa ashehadou anna mohammadane abdouhou wa rassoulouhou »
And I bear witness that Muhammad is His slave and Prophet

حي على الصلاة حي على الفلاح
« hayya alaa ssalaati, hayya halaa lfalaahi »
Come to prayer, come to success

قد قامت الصلاة
«qade qaamati ssalaatou»
Prayer has been established,

الله أكبر الله أكبر
«allaahou akbar , allaahou akbar. »
Allah is Great, Allah is Great

لا إلاه إلا الله
« laa ilaaha illa llaah »
there is no god but Allah.

Then, start your prayer by saying:

الله أكبر

« allaahou akbar »

Allah is Great

- Look at the following image -

الله أكبر
Allah is Great
« allaahou akbar »

Then, recite silently surah Al-Fatiha:

بإسم الله الرحمان الرحيم
« bismillaahi rrahmaani rrahiime »
In the name of Allah, Most Gracious, Most Merciful.

الْحَمْدُ لِلَّهِ رَبِّ الْعَالَمِينَ
« alhamdou lillaahi rabbi al-aalamiina »
Praise be to Allah, the Cherisher and Sustainer of the worlds,

الرَّحْمَٰنِ الرَّحِيمِ
« arrahmaani rrahiime »
Most Gracious, Most Merciful,

مَالِكِ يَوْمِ الدِّينِ
« maaliki yawemi ddiine »
Master of the Day of Judgment.

إِيَّاكَ نَعْبُدُ وَإِيَّاكَ نَسْتَعِينُ
« iyyaaka na-aboudo wa iyyaaka nasta-aaiine »
Thee do we worship, and Thine aid we seek.

اهْدِنَا الصِّرَاطَ الْمُسْتَقِيمَ
« ihdina ssiraata almoustaqiime »
Show us the straight way,

»صِرَاطَ الَّذِينَ أَنْعَمْتَ عَلَيْهِمْ غَيْرِ الْمَغْضُوبِ عَلَيْهِمْ وَلَا الضَّالِّينَ. امين.
« siraata lladiina ane-aameta aalayehime, ghayri almaghdoubi aalayehime, wala ddaliine. Amiiiiine »
The way of those on whom Thou hast bestowed Thy Grace, those whose (portion) is not wrath, and who go not astray. Amine.

After finishing ALFATIHA, recite silently any verse from the Quran: For example: Surah AL IKHLAS

باسم الله الرحمن الرحيم
« bismillaahi rrahmaani rrahiime »
In the Name of Allâh, the Most Beneficent, the Most Merciful.

قُلْ هُوَ اللَّهُ أَحَدٌ
« qoul houa llaahou ahade »
Say "Allâh is (the) One

اللَّهُ الصَّمَدُ
« allaahou ssamade »
The Self-Sufficient Master

لَمْ يَلِدْ وَلَمْ يُولَدْ
« lame yalide walame youlade »
"He begets not, nor was He begotten.

وَلَمْ يَكُنْ لَهُ كُفُوًا أَحَدٌ
« walame yakoune lahou koufou-ane ahade »
And there is none co-equal or comparable unto Him.

Then, say: :

الله أكبر

« allaahou akbar »

Allah is Great

> الله أكبر
> **Allah is Great**
> « allaahou akbar »

And, do as in the following image:

Then, say three times :

"subhaana rabiyya al-aaddiime » :

سبحان ربي العظيم

Glory be to my God

Then, standing upright again and saying:

"sami-aa llaahou liman hamidah" سمع الله لمن حمده

« Allah listens to those who praise Him »

« rabbanaa walaka lhamd » ربنا و لك الحمد

Praise be to our God

Then, say: :

الله أكبر

« allaahou akbar »

Allah is Great

الله أكبر
Allah is Great
« allaahou akbar »

While prostrating, you have to say 3 times :

"subhaana rabiyya al-aalaa"

سبحان ربي الأعلى

Glory to my God

Raising the head and saying:

"Allaahou akbar"

الله أكبر

Allah is Great

Then, say a request such as :

اللهم إغفر لي و إرحمني

« Allaahoumaa ighfir lii wa rhamnii »

My God, forgive me and have mercy on me

Then slowly bending down to prostrate and saying:

"Allaahou akbar"

الله أكبر

Allah is Great

Once again, while prostrating you have to say 3 times :

"subhaana rabiyya al-aalaa"

سبحان ربي الأعلى

Glory to my God

THE SECOND « RAKAAH »

This is the illustration of the second « RAKAAH »

Then, stand up again, your face towards the QIBLA, MECCA

Then, start your second RAKAAH by saying:

الله أكبر

« allaahou akbar »

Allah is Great

- Look at the following image -

Then, recite once again surah silently Al-Fatiha:

بإسم الله الرحمان الرحيم
« bismillaahi rrahmaani rrahiime »
In the name of Allah, Most Gracious, Most Merciful.

الْحَمْدُ لِلَّهِ رَبِّ الْعَالَمِينَ
« alhamdou lillaahi rabbi al-aalamiine »
Praise be to Allah, the Cherisher and Sustainer of the worlds,

الرَّحْمَٰنِ الرَّحِيمِ
« arrahmaani rrahiime »
Most Gracious, Most Merciful,

مَالِكِ يَوْمِ الدِّينِ
« maaliki yawemi ddiine »
Master of the Day of Judgment.

إِيَّاكَ نَعْبُدُ وَإِيَّاكَ نَسْتَعِينُ
« iyyaaka na-aboudo wa iyyaaka nasta-aaiine »
Thee do we worship, and Thine aid we seek.

اهْدِنَا الصِّرَاطَ الْمُسْتَقِيمَ
« ihdina ssiraata almoustaqiime »
Show us the straight way,

»صِرَاطَ الَّذِينَ أَنْعَمْتَ عَلَيْهِمْ غَيْرِ الْمَغْضُوبِ عَلَيْهِمْ وَلَا الضَّالِّينَ. امين.
« siraata lladina ane-aameta aalayehime, ghayri almaghdoubi aalayehime, wala ddaliine. Amiiiiine »
The way of those on whom Thou hast bestowed Thy Grace, those whose (portion) is not wrath, and who go not astray. Amine.

After finishing ALFATIHA, recite silently any verse from the Quran:
For example: سورة النصر *Surah An-Nasr*

بسم الله الرحمن الرحيم
« bismillaahi rrahmaani rrahiime »
In the Name of Allâh, the Most Beneficent, the Most Merciful.

إِذَا جَاءَ نَصْرُ اللَّهِ وَالْفَتْحُ
« idaa jaa a nasrou llaahi walfatehou »
When comes the Help of Allah, and Victory,

وَرَأَيْتَ النَّاسَ يَدْخُلُونَ فِي دِينِ اللَّهِ أَفْوَاجًا
« wa ra-ayeta nnaasa yadkhoulouna fii diini llaahi afwaajane »
And thou dost see the people enter Allah's Religion in crowds,

فَسَبِّحْ بِحَمْدِ رَبِّكَ وَاسْتَغْفِرْهُ إِنَّهُ كَانَ تَوَّابًا
« fasabbih bismi rabbika wa staghfirhou innahou kaana tawaabane »
Celebrate the praises of thy Lord, and pray for His Forgiveness: For He is Oft-Returning (in Grace and Mercy).

Then, say: :

الله أكبر

« allaahou akbar »

Allah is Great

الله أكبر
Allah is Great
« allaahou akbar »

And, do as in the following image:

Then, say three times :

"subhaana rabiyya al-aaddiime » :

سبحان ربي العظيم

Glory be to my God

Then, standing upright again and saying:

"sami-aa llaahou limane hamidah" سمع الله لمن حمده

« Allah listens to those who praise Him »

« rabbanaa walaka lhamd » ربنا و لك الحمد

Praise be to our God

Then, say: :

الله أكبر

« allaahou akbar »

Allah is Great

> الله أكبر
> **Allah is Great**
> « allaahou akbar »

While prostrating, you have to say three times :

"subhaana rabiyya al-aalaa"

سبحان ربي الأعلى

Glory to my God

Raising the head and saying:

"Allaahou akbar"

الله أكبر

Allah is Great

الله أكبر
Allah is Great
« allaahou akbar »

Then, say a request such as :

اللهم إغفر لي و إرحمني

« Allaahoumma ighfir lii wa rhamenii »

My God, forgive me and have mercy on me

Then slowly bending down to prostrate and saying:

"Allaahou akbar"

الله أكبر

Allah is Great

الله أكبر
Allah is Great
« allaahou akbar »

Once again, while prostrating you have to say 3 times :

"subhaana rabiyya al-aalaa"

سبحان ربي الأعلى

Glory to my God

Raising the head and saying:

"Allaahou akbar"

الله أكبر

Allah is Great

الله أكبر
Allah is Great
« allaahou akbar »

Then, you sit on your knees to recite the tashahhud while moving your finger of your right hand:

التحيات لله و الصلوات و الطيبات،
« attahiyaatou lillaah wa ssalawaatou wa ttayibaate »
All compliments, prayers and pure words are due to Allaah.

السلام عليك أيها النبي ، و رحمة الله و بركاته
«assalaamou aalayeka ayouha nnabii warahmatou llaahi wa barakaatouhou »
Peace be upon you, O Prophet, and the mercy of Allaah and His blessings.

السلام علينا و على عباد الله الصالحين،
« assalaamou aalayenaa wa aalaa aibaadi llahi ssaalihiina »
Peace be upon us and upon the righteous slaves of Allaah.

أشهد أن لا إله إلا الله،
« ashehadou anna laa ilaaha illa llaah »
I bear witness that there is no god except Allaah

.و أشهد أن محمدا عبده و رسوله
«wa ashehadou anna mouhammadane aabedouhou wa rasoulouhou »
and I bear witness that Muhammad is His slave and Messenger

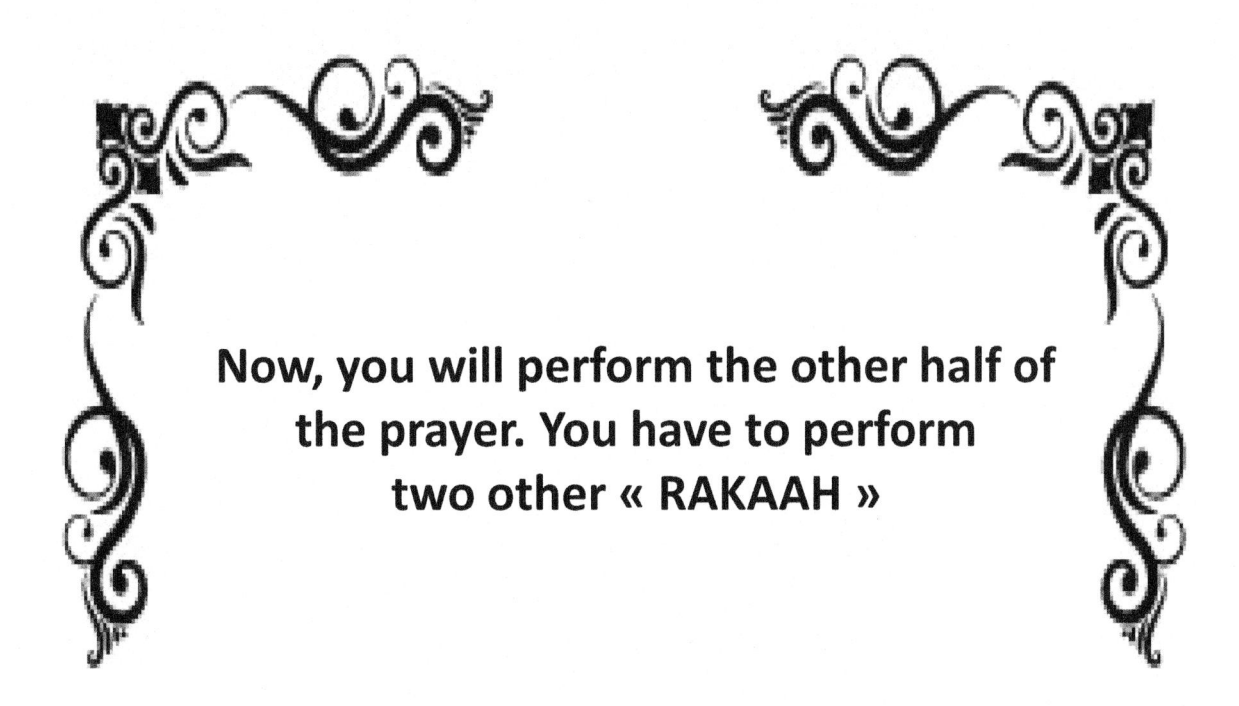

Now, you will perform the other half of the prayer. You have to perform two other « RAKAAH »

THE THIRD RAKAAH

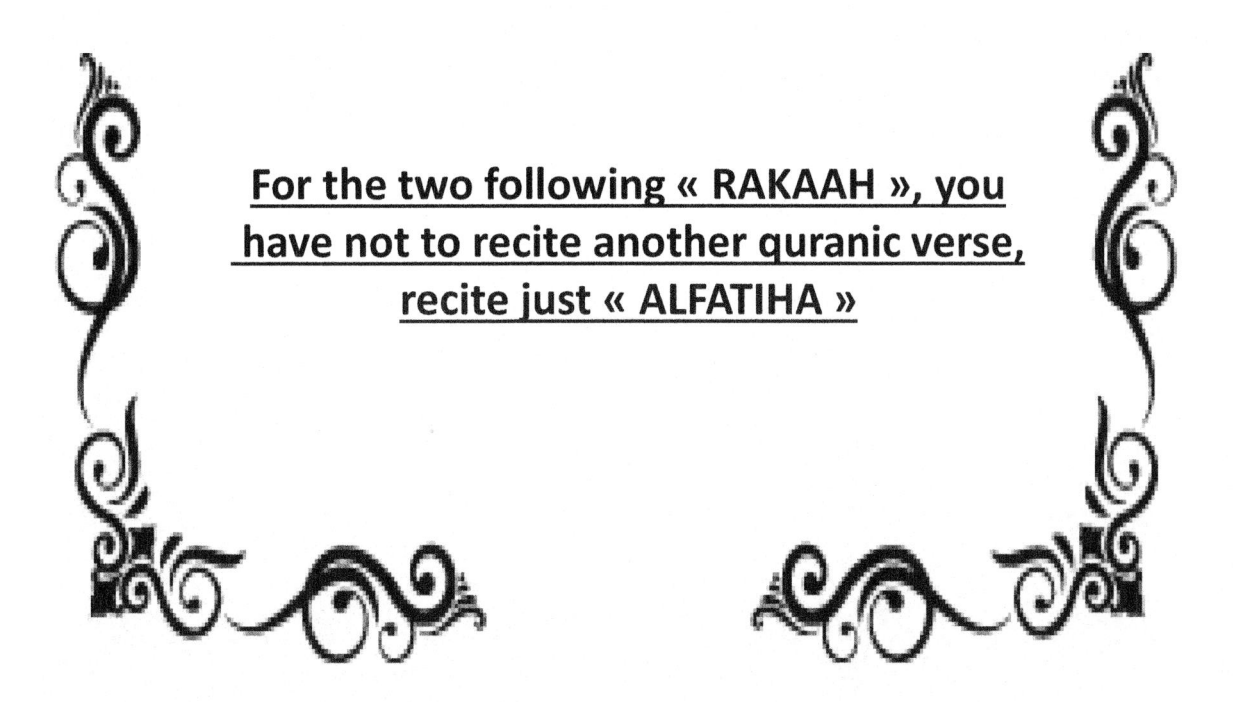

For the two following « RAKAAH », you have not to recite another quranic verse, recite just « ALFATIHA »

This is the illustration of the third « RAKAAH »

Then, start your third « RAKAAH» by saying:

الله أكبر

« allaahou akbar »

Allah is Great

- Look at the following image -

الله أكبر
Allah is Great
« allaahou akbar »

Then, recite again silently surah Al-Fatiha:

بإسم الله الرحمان الرحيم
« bismillaahi rrahmaani rrahiime »
In the name of Allah, Most Gracious, Most Merciful.

الْحَمْدُ لِلَّهِ رَبِّ الْعَالَمِينَ
« alhamdou lilaahi rabbi al-aalamiine »
Praise be to Allah, the Cherisher and Sustainer of the worlds,

الرَّحْمَنِ الرَّحِيمِ
« arrahmaani rrahiime »
Most Gracious, Most Merciful,

مَالِكِ يَوْمِ الدِّينِ
« maaliki yawemi ddiine »
Master of the Day of Judgment.

إِيَّاكَ نَعْبُدُ وَإِيَّاكَ نَسْتَعِينُ
« iyyaaka na-aboudo wa iyyaaka nasta-aaiine »
Thee do we worship, and Thine aid we seek.

اهْدِنَا الصِّرَاطَ الْمُسْتَقِيمَ
« ihdina ssiraata almoustaqiime »
Show us the straight way,

»صِرَاطَ الَّذِينَ أَنْعَمْتَ عَلَيْهِمْ غَيْرِ الْمَغْضُوبِ عَلَيْهِمْ وَلَا الضَّالِّينَ. امين.
« siraata lladina ane-aameta aalayehime, ghayri almaghdoubi
 aalayehime, wala ddaliine. Amiiiiine »
The way of those on whom Thou hast bestowed Thy Grace, those whose (portion) is not wrath, and who go not astray. Amine.

Then, say: :

الله أكبر

« allaahou akbar »

Allah is Great

الله أكبر
Allah is Great
« allaahou akbar »

And, do as in the following image:

Then, say three times :

"subhaana rabiyya al-aaddiime » :

سبحان ربي العظيم

Glory be to my God

Then, standing upright again and saying:

"sami-aa llaahou liman hamidah" سمع الله لمن حمده

« Allah listens to those who praise Him »

« rabbanaa walaka lhamd » ربنا و لك الحمد

Praise be to our God

Then, say:

اللهُ أكبر

« allaahou akbar »

Allah is Great

اللهُ أكبر
Allah is Great
« allaahou akbar »

While prostrating, you have to say 3 times :

"subhaana rabiyya al-aalaa"

سبحان ربي الأعلى

Glory to my God

Raising the head and saying:

"Allaahou akbar"

الله أكبر

Allah is Great

الله أكبر
Allah is Great
« allaahou akbar »

Then, say a request such as :

اللهم إغفر لي و إرحمني

« Allaahouma ighfir lii wa rhamnii »

My God, forgive me and have mercy on me

Then slowly bending down to prostrate and saying:

"Allaahou akbar"

الله أكبر

Allah is Great

الله أكبر
Allah is Great
« allaahou akbar »

Once again, while prostrating you have to say 3 times :

"subhaana rabiyya al-aalaa"

سبحان ربي الأعلى

Glory to my God

FOURTH RAKAAH

This is the illustration of the fourth « RAKAAH »

Then, start your fourth « RAKAAH» by saying:

الله أكبر

« allaahou akbar »

Allah is Great

- Look at the following image -

الله أكبر

Allah is Great

« allaahou akbar »

Then, recite once again surah Al-Fatiha:

بِإسم الله الرحمان الرحيم
« bismillaahi rrahmaani rrahiime »
In the name of Allah, Most Gracious, Most Merciful.

الْحَمْدُ لِلَّهِ رَبِّ الْعَالَمِينَ
« alhamdou lilaahi rabbi al-aalamiine »
Praise be to Allah, the Cherisher and Sustainer of the worlds,

الرَّحْمٰنِ الرَّحِيمِ
« arrahmaani rrahiime »
Most Gracious, Most Merciful,

مَالِكِ يَوْمِ الدِّينِ
« maaliki yawemi ddiine »
Master of the Day of Judgment.

إِيَّاكَ نَعْبُدُ وَإِيَّاكَ نَسْتَعِينُ
« iyyaaka na-aaboudo wa iyyaaka nasta-aaiine »
Thee do we worship, and Thine aid we seek.

اهْدِنَا الصِّرَاطَ الْمُسْتَقِيمَ
« ihdinaa ssiraata almoustaqiime »
Show us the straight way,

«صِرَاطَ الَّذِينَ أَنْعَمْتَ عَلَيْهِمْ غَيْرِ الْمَغْضُوبِ عَلَيْهِمْ وَلَا الضَّالِّينَ. امين.
« siraata lladina ane-aameta aalayehime, ghayri almaghdoubi aalayehime, wala ddaliine. Amiiiiine »
The way of those on whom Thou hast bestowed Thy Grace, those whose (portion) is not wrath, and who go not astray. Amine.

Then, say: :

الله أكبر

« allaahou akbar »

Allah is Great

الله أكبر
Allah is Great
« allaahou akbar »

And, do as in the following image:

Then, say three times :

"subhaana rabiyya al-aaddiime » :

سبحان ربي العظيم

Glory be to my God

Then, standing upright again and saying:

"sami-aa llaahou limane hamidah" سمع الله لمن حمده

« Allah listens to those who praise Him »

« rabbanaa walaka lhamd » ربنا و لك الحمد

Praise be to our God

Then, say: :

الله أكبر

« allaahou akbar »

Allah is Great

الله أكبر
Allah is Great
« allaahou akbar »

While prostrating, you have to say 3 times :

"subhaana rabiyya al-aalaa"

سبحان ربي الأعلى

Glory to my God

Raising the head and saying:

"Allaahou akbar"

الله أكبر

Allah is Great

Allah is Great
« allaahou akbar »

الله أكبر

Then, say a request such as :

اللهم إغفر لي و إرحمني

« Allaahouma ighfir lii wa rhamnii »

My God, forgive me and have mercy on me

Then slowly bending down to prostrate and saying:

"Allaahou akbar"

الله أكبر

Allah is Great

الله أكبر
Allah is Great
« allaahou akbar »

Once again, while prostrating you have to say 3 times :

"subhaana rabiyya al-aalaa"

سبحان ربي الأعلى

Glory to my God

Raising the head and saying:

"Allaahou akbar"

الله أكبر

Allah is Great

الله أكبر
Allah is Great
« allaahou akbar »

Then, you sit on your knees to recite the tashahhud and Ibrahimya prayer, while moving your finger of your right hand:
(as written on the following page)

The Tashahhud and Ibrahimya prayer:

التحيات لله و الصلوات و الطيبات،
« attahiyaatou lillaah wa ssalawaatou wa ttayibaate »
All compliments, prayers and pure words are due to Allaah.

السلام عليك أيها النبي ، و رحمة الله و بركاته
«assalaamou aalayeka ayouha nnabii warahmatou llaahi wa barakaatouhou »
Peace be upon you, O Prophet, and the mercy of Allaah and His blessings.

السلام علينا و على عباد الله الصالحين،
« assalaamou aalayenaa wa aalaa aibaadi llaahi ssaalihiina »
Peace be upon us and upon the righteous slaves of Allaah.

أشهد أن لا إله إلا الله،
« ashehadou anna laa ilaaha illa llaah »
I bear witness that there is no god except Allaah

و أشهد أن محمدا عبده و رسوله.
«wa ashehadou anna mouhammadane aabedouhou wa rasoulouhou »
and I bear witness that Muhammad is His slave and Messenger.

اللهم صلي على محمد و على آل محمد
« allahoumma salli aalaa mouhammadine wa aalaa aali mouhammadine »
O Allaah, send prayers upon Muhammad and upon the family of Muhammad,

كما صليت على إبراهيم و على آل إبراهيم
« kamaa sallayeta aalaa ibrahiim wa aalaa aali ibrahiim »
as You sent prayers upon Ibraaheem and the family of Ibraaheem,

وبارك على محمد و على آل محمد
« wa baarik aalaa mouhammadine wa aalaa aali mouhammadine »
O Allaah, bless Muhammad and the family of Muhammad

كما باركت على إبراهيم و على آل إبراهيم
« kamaa baarakta aalaa ibrahiim wa aalaa aali ibrahiim »
as You blessed Ibraaheem and the family of Ibraaheem,

في العالمين إنك حميد مجيد.
« fii l aalamiina innaka hamiidoune majiide »
You are indeed Worthy of Praise, Full of Glory.

The termination of the prayers takes place as follows:

The head is turned to the right and you say:

"Assalaamou aalaykoum wa rahmatou llaahi ta-aalaa wa barakaatouh"

السلام عليكم و رحمة الله تعالى و بركاته

Peace, mercy and blessings of Almighty God

Then the head is turned to the left and you say:

"Assalaamou aalaykoum wa rahmatou llaahi ta-aalaa wa barakaatouh"

السلام عليكم و رحمة الله تعالى و بركاته

Peace, mercy and blessings of Almighty God

After finishing your prayer,
you can say your request « Dua »

Surah AL Mumtahina : سورة الممتحنة

رَبَّنَا لَا تَجْعَلْنَا فِتْنَةً لِلَّذِينَ كَفَرُوا وَاغْفِرْ لَنَا رَبَّنَا إِنَّكَ أَنْتَ الْعَزِيزُ الْحَكِيمُ (5)

« rabbanaa laa taj-alnaa fitnatane lilladiina kafarou wa ghfire lanaa, rabbanaa innaka aneta l-azizou lhakimou. »

"Our Lord. Make us not a trial for the Unbelievers, but forgive us, our Lord. for Thou art the Exalted in Might, the Wise."

HOW TO PRAY
SALAT AL-AASER

Number of Rakaahs:
Four Rakaahs.

Recitation of the Quran:
Both boys and girls have to recite silently.

Time:
The late part of the afternoon

So, let's start.

بإسم الله الرحمان الرحيم
« bismi llaahi rrahmaani rrahiime »
In the name of Allah, Most Gracious, Most Merciful.

This is the illustration of the first « RAKAAH »

First, stand up, your face towards QIBLA, MECCA

Then, always start with « bismillaah »: in the name of Allah.

You should have the intention to pray and then say:

الله أكبر الله أكبر

«Allaahou akbar, allaahou akbar.»

Allah is Great, Allah is Great

أشهد أن لا إلاه إلا الله

« ashehadou anna laa ilaaha illa llaah »

I bear witness that there is no god but Allah

وأشهد أن محمدا عبده و رسوله

« wa ashehadou anna mohammadane abdouhou wa rassoulouhou »

And I bear witness that Muhammad is His slave and Prophet

حي على الصلاة حي على الفلاح

« hayya alaa ssalaati, hayya halaa lfalaahi »

Come to prayer, come to success

قد قامت الصلاة

«qade qaamati ssalaatou»

Prayer has been established,

الله أكبر الله أكبر

«allaahou akbar , allaahou akbar. »

Allah is Great, Allah is Great

لا إلاه إلا الله

« laa ilaaha illa llaah »

there is no god but Allah.

Then, start your prayer by saying:

الله أكبر

« allaahou akbar »

Allah is Great

- Look at the following image -

> الله أكبر
> **Allah is Great**
> « allaahou akbar »

Then, recite silently surah Al-Fatiha:

بإسم الله الرحمان الرحيم
« bismillaahi rrahmaani rrahiime »
In the name of Allah, Most Gracious, Most Merciful.

الْحَمْدُ لِلَّهِ رَبِّ الْعَالَمِينَ
« alhamdou lillaahi rabbi al-aalamiina »
Praise be to Allah, the Cherisher and Sustainer of the worlds,

الرَّحْمَٰنِ الرَّحِيمِ
« arrahmaani rrahiime »
Most Gracious, Most Merciful,

مَالِكِ يَوْمِ الدِّينِ
« maaliki yawemi ddiine »
Master of the Day of Judgment.

إِيَّاكَ نَعْبُدُ وَإِيَّاكَ نَسْتَعِينُ
« iyyaaka na-aboudo wa iyyaaka nasta-aaiine »
Thee do we worship, and Thine aid we seek.

اهْدِنَا الصِّرَاطَ الْمُسْتَقِيمَ
« ihdina ssiraata almoustaqiime »
Show us the straight way,

»صِرَاطَ الَّذِينَ أَنْعَمْتَ عَلَيْهِمْ غَيْرِ الْمَغْضُوبِ عَلَيْهِمْ وَلَا الضَّالِّينَ. امين.
« siraata lladiina ane-aameta aalayehime, ghayri almaghdoubi aalayehime, wala ddaliine. Amiiiiine »
The way of those on whom Thou hast bestowed Thy Grace, those whose (portion) is not wrath, and who go not astray. Amine.

After finishing ALFATIHA, recite silently any verse from the Quran: For example: Surah AL IKHLAS

بسم الله الرحمن الرحيم
« bismillaahi rrahmaani rrahiime »
In the Name of Allâh, the Most Beneficent, the Most Merciful.

قُلْ هُوَ اللَّهُ أَحَدٌ
« qoul houa llaahou ahade »
Say "Allâh is (the) One

اللَّهُ الصَّمَدُ
« allaahou ssamade »
The Self-Sufficient Master

لَمْ يَلِدْ وَلَمْ يُولَدْ
« lame yalide walame youlade »
"He begets not, nor was He begotten.

وَلَمْ يَكُنْ لَهُ كُفُوًا أَحَدٌ
« walame yakoune lahou koufou-ane ahade »
And there is none co-equal or comparable unto Him.

Then, say: :

الله أكبر

« allaahou akbar »

Allah is Great

> الله أكبر
> **Allah is Great**
> « allaahou akbar »

And, do as in the following image:

Then, say three times :

"subhaana rabiyya al-aaddiime » :

سبحان ربي العظيم

Glory be to my God

Then, standing upright again and saying:

"sami-aa llaahou liman hamidah" سمع الله لمن حمده

« Allah listens to those who praise Him »

« rabbanaa walaka lhamd » ربنا و لك الحمد

Praise be to our God

Then, say: :

الله أكبر

« allaahou akbar »

Allah is Great

> الله أكبر
> **Allah is Great**
> « allaahou akbar »

While prostrating, you have to say 3 times :

"subhaana rabiyya al-aalaa"

سبحان ربي الأعلى

Glory to my God

Raising the head and saying:

"Allaahou akbar"

الله أكبر

Allah is Great

Then, say a request such as :

اللهم إغفر لي و إرحمني

« Allaahoumaa ighfir lii wa rhamnii »

My God, forgive me and have mercy on me

Then slowly bending down to prostrate and saying:

"Allaahou akbar"

الله أكبر

Allah is Great

Once again, while prostrating you have to say 3 times :

"subhaana rabiyya al-aalaa"

سبحان ربي الأعلى

Glory to my God

THE SECOND « RAKAAH »

This is the illustration of the second « RAKAAH »

Then, stand up again, your face towards the QIBLA, MECCA

Then, start your second RAKAAH by saying:

الله أكبر

« allaahou akbar »

Allah is Great

- **Look at the following image** -

Then, recite once again surah silently Al-Fatiha:

بإسم الله الرحمان الرحيم
« bismillaahi rrahmaani rrahiime »
In the name of Allah, Most Gracious, Most Merciful.

الْحَمْدُ لِلَّهِ رَبِّ الْعَالَمِينَ
« alhamdou lillaahi rabbi al-aalamiine »
Praise be to Allah, the Cherisher and Sustainer of the worlds,

الرَّحْمَٰنِ الرَّحِيمِ
« arrahmaani rrahiime »
Most Gracious, Most Merciful,

مَالِكِ يَوْمِ الدِّينِ
« maaliki yawemi ddiine »
Master of the Day of Judgment.

إِيَّاكَ نَعْبُدُ وَإِيَّاكَ نَسْتَعِينُ
« iyyaaka na-aboudo wa iyyaaka nasta-aaiine »
Thee do we worship, and Thine aid we seek.

اهْدِنَا الصِّرَاطَ الْمُسْتَقِيمَ
« ihdina ssiraata almoustaqiime »
Show us the straight way,

»صِرَاطَ الَّذِينَ أَنْعَمْتَ عَلَيْهِمْ غَيْرِ الْمَغْضُوبِ عَلَيْهِمْ وَلَا الضَّالِّينَ. امين.
« siraata lladina ane-aameta aalayehime, ghayri almaghdoubi aalayehime, wala ddaliine. Amiiiiine »
The way of those on whom Thou hast bestowed Thy Grace, those whose (portion) is not wrath, and who go not astray. Amine.

After finishing ALFATIHA, recite silently any verse from the Quran:
For example: سورة النصر *Surah An-Nasr*

بـاسم الله الرحمن الرحيم

« bismillaahi rrahmaani rrahiime »

In the Name of Allâh, the Most Beneficent, the Most Merciful.

إِذَا جَاءَ نَصْرُ اللَّهِ وَالْفَتْحُ

« idaa jaa a nasrou llaahi walfatehou »

When comes the Help of Allah, and Victory,

وَرَأَيْتَ النَّاسَ يَدْخُلُونَ فِي دِينِ اللَّهِ أَفْوَاجًا

« wa ra-ayeta nnaasa yadkhoulouna fii diini llaahi afwaajane »

And thou dost see the people enter Allah's Religion in crowds,

فَسَبِّحْ بِحَمْدِ رَبِّكَ وَاسْتَغْفِرْهُ إِنَّهُ كَانَ تَوَّابًا

« fasabbih bismi rabbika wa staghfirhou innahou kaana tawaabane »

Celebrate the praises of thy Lord, and pray for His Forgiveness: For He is Oft-Returning (in Grace and Mercy).

Then, say: :

الله أكبر

« allaahou akbar »

Allah is Great

الله أكبر
Allah is Great
« allaahou akbar »

And, do as in the following image:

Then, say three times :

"subhaana rabiyya al-aaddiime » :

سبحان ربي العظيم

Glory be to my God

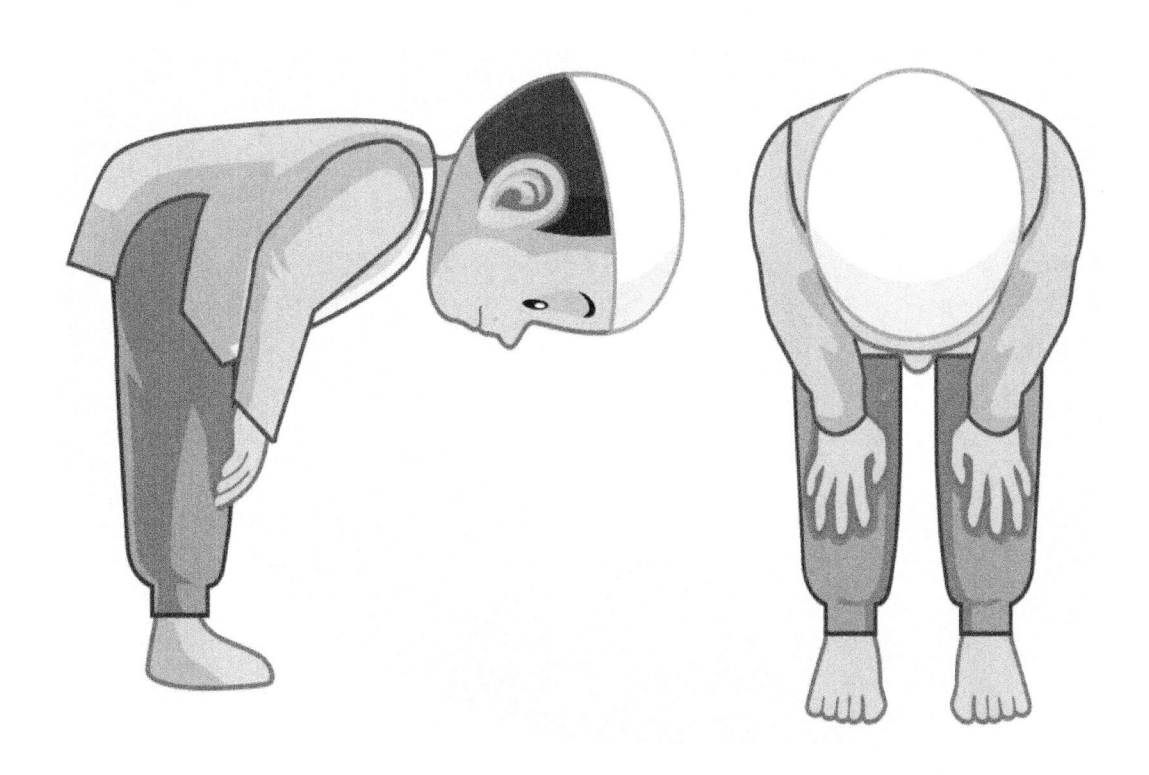

Then, standing upright again and saying:

"sami-aa llaahou limane hamidah" سمع الله لمن حمده

« Allah listens to those who praise Him »

« rabbanaa walaka lhamd » ربنا و لك الحمد

Praise be to our God

Then, say: :

الله أكبر

« allaahou akbar »

Allah is Great

الله أكبر
Allah is Great
« allaahou akbar »

While prostrating, you have to say three times :

"subhaana rabiyya al-aalaa"

سبحان ربي الأعلى

Glory to my God

Raising the head and saying:

"Allaahou akbar"

الله أكبر

Allah is Great

الله أكبر
Allah is Great
« allaahou akbar »

Then, say a request such as :

اللهم إغفر لي و إرحمني

« Allaahoumma ighfir lii wa rhamenii »

My God, forgive me and have mercy on me

Then slowly bending down to prostrate and saying:

"Allaahou akbar"

الله أكبر

Allah is Great

الله أكبر
Allah is Great
« allaahou akbar »

Once again, while prostrating you have to say 3 times :

"subhaana rabiyya al-aalaa"

سبحان ربي الأعلى

Glory to my God

Raising the head and saying:

"Allaahou akbar"

الله أكبر

Allah is Great

الله أكبر
Allah is Great
« allaahou akbar »

Then, you sit on your knees to recite the tashahhud while moving your finger of your right hand:

التحيات لله و الصلوات و الطيبات،
« attahiyaatou lillaah wa ssalawaatou wa ttayibaate »
All compliments, prayers and pure words are due to Allaah.

السلام عليك أيها النبي ، و رحمة الله و بركاته
«assalaamou aalayeka ayouha nnabii warahmatou llaahi wa barakaatouhou »
Peace be upon you, O Prophet, and the mercy of Allaah and His blessings.

السلام علينا و على عباد الله الصالحين،
« assalaamou aalayenaa wa aalaa aibaadi llahi ssaalihiina »
Peace be upon us and upon the righteous slaves of Allaah.

أشهد أن لا إله إلا الله،
« ashehadou anna laa ilaaha illa llaah »
I bear witness that there is no god except Allaah

و أشهد أن محمدا عبده و رسوله.
«wa ashehadou anna mouhammadane aabedouhou wa rasoulouhou »
and I bear witness that Muhammad is His slave and Messenger

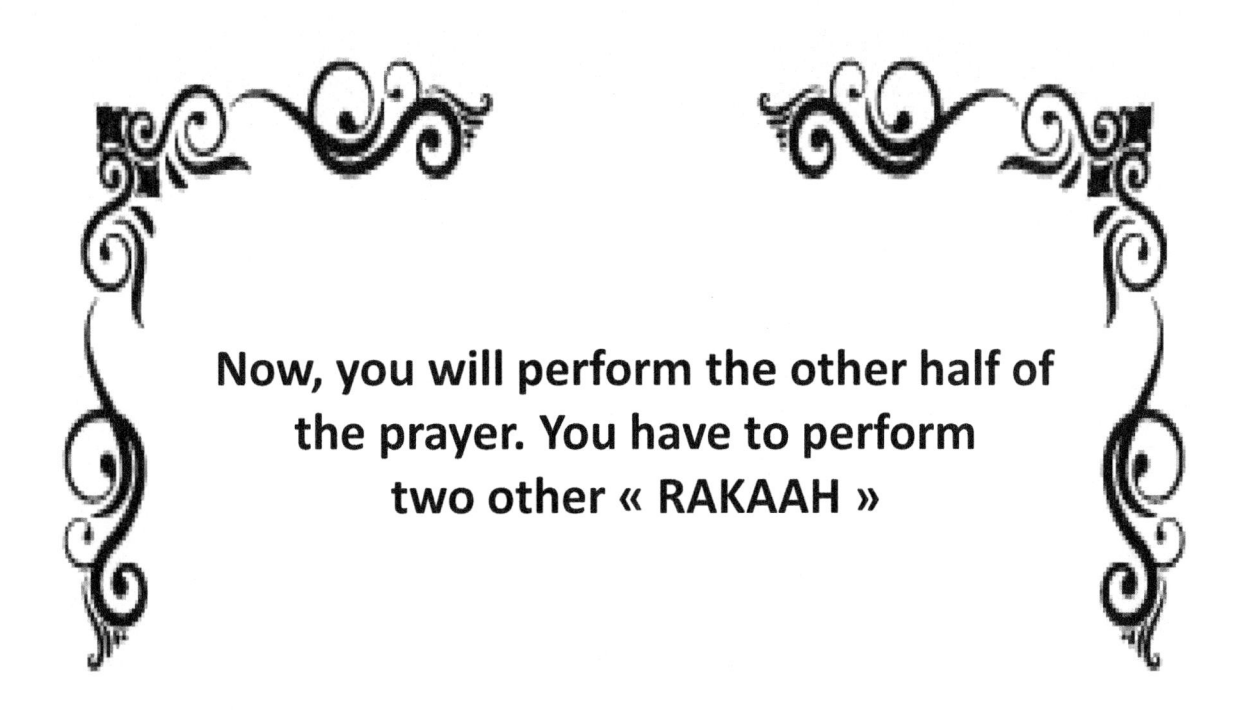

Now, you will perform the other half of the prayer. You have to perform two other « RAKAAH »

THE THIRD RAKAAH

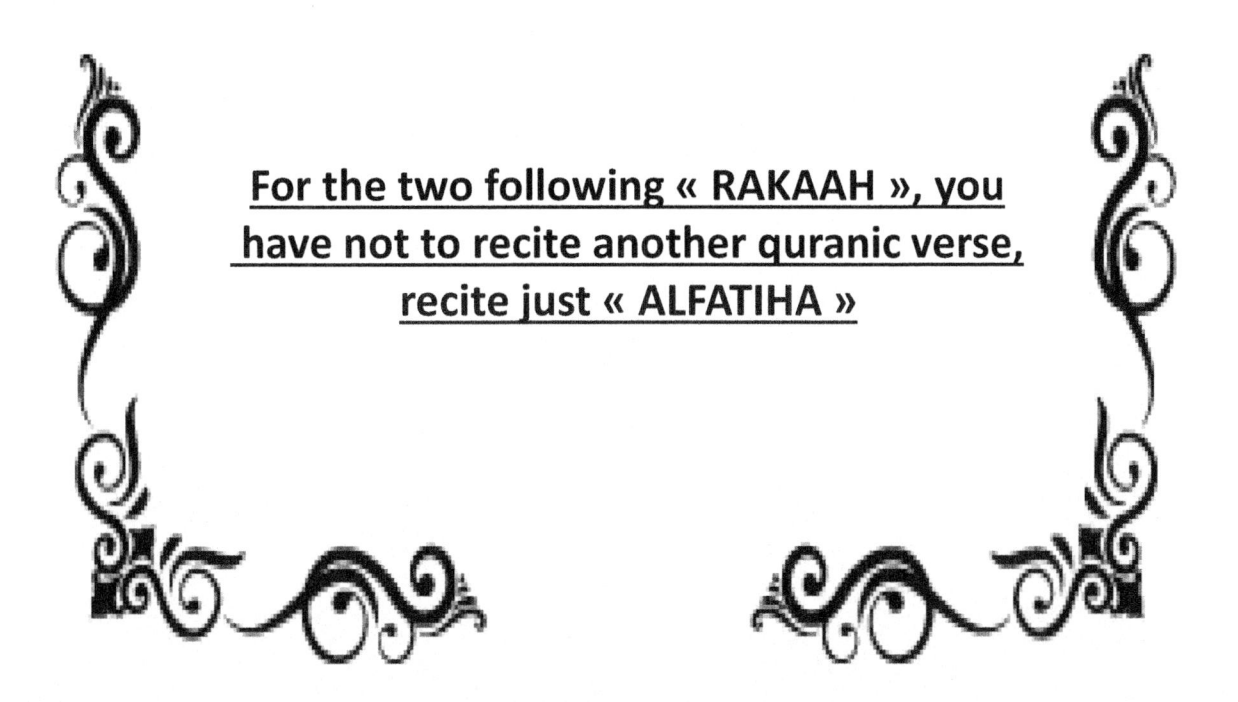

For the two following « RAKAAH », you have not to recite another quranic verse, recite just « ALFATIHA »

This is the illustration of the third « RAKAAH »

Then, start your third « RAKAAH» by saying:

الله أكبر

« allaahou akbar »

Allah is Great

- Look at the following image -

الله أكبر

Allah is Great

« allaahou akbar »

Then, recite again silently surah Al-Fatiha:

بإسم الله الرحمان الرحيم
« bismillaahi rrahmaani rrahiime »
In the name of Allah, Most Gracious, Most Merciful.

الْحَمْدُ لِلَّهِ رَبِّ الْعَالَمِينَ
« alhamdou lilaahi rabbi al-aalamiine »
Praise be to Allah, the Cherisher and Sustainer of the worlds,

الرَّحْمَٰنِ الرَّحِيمِ
« arrahmaani rrahiime »
Most Gracious, Most Merciful,

مَالِكِ يَوْمِ الدِّينِ
« maaliki yawemi ddiine »
Master of the Day of Judgment.

إِيَّاكَ نَعْبُدُ وَإِيَّاكَ نَسْتَعِينُ
« iyyaaka na-aboudo wa iyyaaka nasta-aaiine »
Thee do we worship, and Thine aid we seek.

اهْدِنَا الصِّرَاطَ الْمُسْتَقِيمَ
« ihdina ssiraata almoustaqiime »
Show us the straight way,

»صِرَاطَ الَّذِينَ أَنْعَمْتَ عَلَيْهِمْ غَيْرِ الْمَغْضُوبِ عَلَيْهِمْ وَلَا الضَّالِّينَ. امين.
« siraata lladina ane-aameta aalayehime, ghayri almaghdoubi
 aalayehime, wala ddaliine. Amiiiiine »
The way of those on whom Thou hast bestowed Thy Grace, those whose (portion) is not wrath, and who go not astray. Amine.

Then, say: :

الله أكبر

« allaahou akbar »

Allah is Great

> الله أكبر
> **Allah is Great**
> « allaahou akbar »

And, do as in the following image:

Then, say three times :

"subhaana rabiyya al-aaddiime » :

سبحان ربي العظيم

Glory be to my God

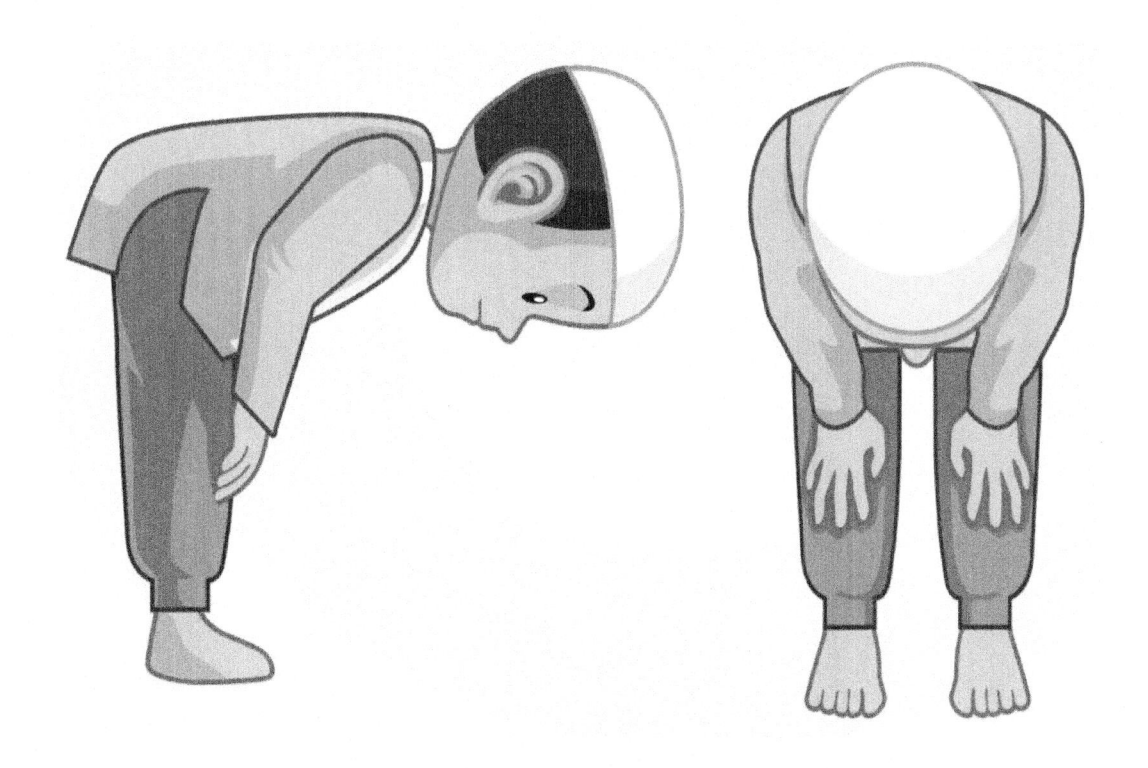

Then, standing upright again and saying:

"sami-aa llaahou liman hamidah" سمع الله لمن حمده

« Allah listens to those who praise Him »

« rabbanaa walaka lhamd » ربنا و لك الحمد

Praise be to our God

Then, say:

الله أكبر

« allaahou akbar »

Allah is Great

> الله أكبر
> **Allah is Great**
> « allaahou akbar »

While prostrating, you have to say 3 times :

"subhaana rabiyya al-aalaa"

سبحان ربي الأعلى

Glory to my God

Raising the head and saying:

"Allaahou akbar"

الله أكبر

Allah is Great

الله أكبر
Allah is Great
« allaahou akbar »

Then, say a request such as :

اللهم إغفر لي و إرحمني

« Allaahouma ighfir lii wa rhamnii »

My God, forgive me and have mercy on me

Then slowly bending down to prostrate and saying:

"Allaahou akbar"

الله أكبر

Allah is Great

الله أكبر
Allah is Great
« allaahou akbar »

Once again, while prostrating you have to say 3 times :

"subhaana rabiyya al-aalaa"

سبحان ربي الأعلى

Glory to my God

FOURTH RAKAAH

This is the illustration of the fourth « RAKAAH »

Then, start your fourth « RAKAAH» by saying:

الله أكبر

« allaahou akbar »

Allah is Great

- Look at the following image -

Then, recite once again silently surah Al-Fatiha:

بِاسْمِ اللهِ الرحمان الرحيم
« bismillaahi rrahmaani rrahiime »
In the name of Allah, Most Gracious, Most Merciful.

الْحَمْدُ لِلَّهِ رَبِّ الْعَالَمِينَ
« alhamdou lilaahi rabbi al-aalamiine »
Praise be to Allah, the Cherisher and Sustainer of the worlds,

الرَّحْمَٰنِ الرَّحِيمِ
« arrahmaani rrahiime »
Most Gracious, Most Merciful,

مَالِكِ يَوْمِ الدِّينِ
« maaliki yawemi ddiine »
Master of the Day of Judgment.

إِيَّاكَ نَعْبُدُ وَإِيَّاكَ نَسْتَعِينُ
« iyyaaka na-aboudo wa iyyaaka nasta-aaiine »
Thee do we worship, and Thine aid we seek.

اهْدِنَا الصِّرَاطَ الْمُسْتَقِيمَ
« ihdinaa ssiraata almoustaqiime »
Show us the straight way,

»صِرَاطَ الَّذِينَ أَنْعَمْتَ عَلَيْهِمْ غَيْرِ الْمَغْضُوبِ عَلَيْهِمْ وَلَا الضَّالِّينَ. امين.
« siraata lladina ane-aameta aalayehime, ghayri almaghdoubi aalayehime, wala ddaliine. Amiiiiine »
The way of those on whom Thou hast bestowed Thy Grace, those whose (portion) is not wrath, and who go not astray. Amine.

Then, say: :

الله أكبر

« allaahou akbar »

Allah is Great

> الله أكبر
> **Allah is Great**
> « allaahou akbar »

And, do as in the following image:

Then, say three times :

"subhaana rabiyya al-aaddiime » :

سبحان ربي العظيم

Glory be to my God

Then, standing upright again and saying:

"sami-aa llaahou limane hamidah" سمع الله لمن حمده

« Allah listens to those who praise Him »

« rabbanaa walaka lhamd » ربنا و لك الحمد

Praise be to our God

Then, say: :

الله أكبر

« allaahou akbar »

Allah is Great

الله أكبر
Allah is Great
« allaahou akbar »

While prostrating, you have to say 3 times :

"subhaana rabiyya al-aalaa"

سبحان ربي الأعلى

Glory to my God

Raising the head and saying:

"Allaahou akbar"

الله أكبر

Allah is Great

الله أكبر
Allah is Great
« allaahou akbar »

Then, say a request such as :

اللهم إغفر لي و إرحمني

« Allaahouma ighfir lii wa rhamnii »

My God, forgive me and have mercy on me

Then slowly bending down to prostrate and saying:

"Allaahou akbar"

الله أكبر

Allah is Great

الله أكبر
Allah is Great
« allaahou akbar »

Once again, while prostrating you have to say 3 times :

"subhaana rabiyya al-aalaa"

سبحان ربي الأعلى

Glory to my God

Raising the head and saying:

"Allaahou akbar"

الله أكبر

Allah is Great

الله أكبر
Allah is Great
« allaahou akbar »

Then, you sit on your knees to recite the tashahhud and Ibrahimya prayer, while moving your finger of your right hand:
(as written on the following page)

The Tashahhud and Ibrahimya prayer:

التحيات لله و الصلوات و الطيبات،
« attahiyaatou lillaah wa ssalawaatou wa ttayibaate »
All compliments, prayers and pure words are due to Allaah.

السلام عليك أيها النبي ، و رحمة الله و بركاته
« assalaamou aalayeka ayouha nnabii warahmatou llaahi wa barakaatouhou »
Peace be upon you, O Prophet, and the mercy of Allaah and His blessings.

السلام علينا و على عباد الله الصالحين،
« assalaamou aalayenaa wa aalaa aibaadi llaahi ssaalihiina »
Peace be upon us and upon the righteous slaves of Allaah.

أشهد أن لا إله إلا الله،
« ashehadou anna laa ilaaha illa llaah »
I bear witness that there is no god except Allaah

و أشهد أن محمدا عبده و رسوله.
« wa ashehadou anna mouhammadane aabedouhou wa rasoulouhou »
and I bear witness that Muhammad is His slave and Messenger.

اللهم صلي على محمد و على آل محمد
« allahoumma salli aalaa mouhammadine wa aalaa aali mouhammadine »
O Allaah, send prayers upon Muhammad and upon the family of Muhammad,

كما صليت على إبراهيم و على آل إبراهيم
« kamaa sallayeta aalaa ibrahiim wa aalaa aali ibrahiim »
as You sent prayers upon Ibraaheem and the family of Ibraaheem

وبارك على محمد و على آل محمد
« wa baarik aalaa mouhammadine wa aalaa aali mouhammadine »
O Allaah, bless Muhammad and the family of Muhammad

كما باركت على إبراهيم و على آل إبراهيم
« kamaa baarakta aalaa ibrahiim wa aalaa aali ibrahiim »
as You blessed Ibraaheem and the family of Ibraaheem,

في العالمين إنك حميد مجيد.
« fii l aalamiina innaka hamiidoune majiide »
You are indeed Worthy of Praise, Full of Glory.

The termination of the prayers takes place as follows:

The head is turned to the right and you say:

"Assalaamou aalaykoum wa rahmatou llaahi ta-aalaa wa barakaatouh"

السلام عليكم و رحمة الله تعالى و بركاته

Peace, mercy and blessings of Almighty God

Then the head is turned to the left and you say:

"Assalaamou aalaykoum wa rahmatou llaahi ta-aalaa wa barakaatouh"

السلام عليكم و رحمة الله تعالى و بركاته

Peace, mercy and blessings of Almighty God

Surah Al-Qasas :سورة القصص

رَبِّ نَجِّنِي مِنَ الْقَوْمِ الظَّالِمِينَ (21)

« rabbi najjinii mina lqawemi ddalimiina. »

« My Lord! Save me from the people who are wrong-doers (Zâlimûn) »

HOW TO PRAY
SALAT AL-MAGHREB

Number of Rakaahs:
Three Rakaahs.

Recitation of the Quran:
-**Boys**: First and the second rakaah: recite aloud, and the third Rakaah: recite silently
-**Girls**: Recite silently during all the three Rakaahs

Time:
Just after sunset

So, let's start.

بإسم الله الرحمان الرحيم
« bismi llaahi rrahmaani rrahiime »
In the name of Allah, Most Gracious, Most Merciful.

This is the illustration of the first « RAKAAH »

First, stand up, your face towards QIBLA, MECCA

Then, always start with « bismillaah »: in the name of Allah.

You should have the intention to pray and then say:

الله أكبر الله أكبر

«Allaahou akbar, allaahou akbar.»

Allah is Great, Allah is Great

أشهد أن لا إلاه إلا الله

« ashehadou anna laa ilaaha illa llaah »

I bear witness that there is no god but Allah

وأشهد أن محمدا عبده و رسوله

« wa ashehadou anna mohammadane abdouhou wa rassoulouhou »

And I bear witness that Muhammad is His slave and Prophet

حي على الصلاة حي على الفلاح

« hayya alaa ssalaati, hayya halaa lfalaahi »

Come to prayer, come to success

قد قامت الصلاة

«qade qaamati ssalaatou»

Prayer has been established,

الله أكبر الله أكبر

«allaahou akbar , allaahou akbar. »

Allah is Great, Allah is Great

لا إلاه إلا الله

« laa ilaaha illa llaah »

there is no god but Allah.

Then, start your prayer by saying:

الله أكبر

« allaahou akbar »

Allah is Great

- Look at the following image -

الله أكبر
Allah is Great
« allaahou akbar »

Then, recite aloud surah Al-Fatiha:

بِإِسم الله الرحمان الرحيم
« bismillaahi rrahmaani rrahiime »
In the name of Allah, Most Gracious, Most Merciful.

الْحَمْدُ لِلَّهِ رَبِّ الْعَالَمِينَ
« alhamdou lillaahi rabbi al-aalamiina »
Praise be to Allah, the Cherisher and Sustainer of the worlds,

الرَّحْمَٰنِ الرَّحِيمِ
« arrahmaani rrahiime »
Most Gracious, Most Merciful,

مَالِكِ يَوْمِ الدِّينِ
« maaliki yawemi ddiine »
Master of the Day of Judgment.

إِيَّاكَ نَعْبُدُ وَإِيَّاكَ نَسْتَعِينُ
« iyyaaka na-aboudo wa iyyaaka nasta-aaiine »
Thee do we worship, and Thine aid we seek.

اهْدِنَا الصِّرَاطَ الْمُسْتَقِيمَ
« ihdina ssiraata almoustaqiime »
Show us the straight way,

»صِرَاطَ الَّذِينَ أَنْعَمْتَ عَلَيْهِمْ غَيْرِ الْمَغْضُوبِ عَلَيْهِمْ وَلَا الضَّالِّينَ. امين.
« siraata lladiina ane-aameta aalayehime, ghayri almaghdoubi aalayehime, wala ddaliine. Amiiiiine »
The way of those on whom Thou hast bestowed Thy Grace, those whose (portion) is not wrath, and who go not astray. Amine.

After finishing ALFATIHA, recite aloud any verse from the Quran: For example: Surah AL IKHLAS

بسم الله الرحمن الرحيم
« bismillaahi rrahmaani rrahiime »
In the Name of Allâh, the Most Beneficent, the Most Merciful.

قُلْ هُوَ اللَّهُ أَحَدٌ
« qoul houa llaahou ahade »
Say "Allâh is (the) One

اللَّهُ الصَّمَدُ
« allaahou ssamade »
The Self-Sufficient Master

لَمْ يَلِدْ وَلَمْ يُولَدْ
« lame yalide walame youlade »
"He begets not, nor was He begotten.

وَلَمْ يَكُنْ لَهُ كُفُوًا أَحَدٌ
« walame yakoune lahou koufou-ane ahade »
And there is none co-equal or comparable unto Him.

Then, say: :

الله أكبر

« allaahou akbar »

Allah is Great

> الله أكبر
> **Allah is Great**
> « allaahou akbar »

And, do as in the following image:

Then, say three times :

"subhaana rabiyya al-aaddiime » :

سبحان ربي العظيم

Glory be to my God

Then, standing upright again and saying:

"sami-aa llaahou liman hamidah" سمع الله لمن حمده

« Allah listens to those who praise Him »

« rabbanaa walaka lhamd » ربنا و لك الحمد

Praise be to our God

Then, say: :

الله أكبر

« allaahou akbar »

Allah is Great

> الله أكبر
> **Allah is Great**
> « allaahou akbar »

While prostrating, you have to say 3 times :

"subhaana rabiyya al-aalaa"

سبحان ربي الأعلى

Glory to my God

Raising the head and saying:

"Allaahou akbar"

الله أكبر

Allah is Great

Then, say a request such as :

اللهم إغفر لي و إرحمني

« Allaahoumaa ighfir lii wa rhamnii »

My God, forgive me and have mercy on me

Then slowly bending down to prostrate and saying:

"Allaahou akbar"

الله أكبر

Allah is Great

Once again, while prostrating you have to say 3 times :

"subhaana rabiyya al-aalaa"

سبحان ربي الأعلى

Glory to my God

THE SECOND « RAKAAH »

This is the illustration of the second « RAKAAH »

Then, stand up again, your face towards the QIBLA, MECCA

Then, start your second RAKAAH by saying:

الله أكبر

« allaahou akbar »

Allah is Great

- Look at the following image -

Then, recite once again aloud Al-Fatiha:

بِإسم الله الرحمان الرحيم
« bismillaahi rrahmaani rrahiime »
In the name of Allah, Most Gracious, Most Merciful.

الْحَمْدُ لِلَّهِ رَبِّ الْعَالَمِينَ
« alhamdou lillaahi rabbi al-aalamiine »
Praise be to Allah, the Cherisher and Sustainer of the worlds,

الرَّحْمَٰنِ الرَّحِيمِ
« arrahmaani rrahiime »
Most Gracious, Most Merciful,

مَالِكِ يَوْمِ الدِّينِ
« maaliki yawemi ddiine »
Master of the Day of Judgment.

إِيَّاكَ نَعْبُدُ وَإِيَّاكَ نَسْتَعِينُ
« iyyaaka na-aboudo wa iyyaaka nasta-aaiine »
Thee do we worship, and Thine aid we seek.

اهْدِنَا الصِّرَاطَ الْمُسْتَقِيمَ
« ihdina ssiraata almoustaqiime »
Show us the straight way,

»صِرَاطَ الَّذِينَ أَنْعَمْتَ عَلَيْهِمْ غَيْرِ الْمَغْضُوبِ عَلَيْهِمْ وَلَا الضَّالِّينَ. امين.
« siraata lladina ane-aameta aalayehime, ghayri almaghdoubi aalayehime, wala ddaliine. Amiiiiine »
The way of those on whom Thou hast bestowed Thy Grace, those whose (portion) is not wrath, and who go not astray. Amine.

After finishing ALFATIHA, recite aloud any verse from the Quran:
For example: سورة النصر *Surah An-Nasr*

بسم الله الرحمن الرحيم
« bismillaahi rrahmaani rrahiime »
In the Name of Allâh, the Most Beneficent, the Most Merciful.

إِذَا جَاءَ نَصْرُ اللهِ وَالْفَتْحُ
« idaa jaa a nasrou llaahi walfatehou »
When comes the Help of Allah, and Victory,

وَرَأَيْتَ النَّاسَ يَدْخُلُونَ فِي دِينِ اللهِ أَفْوَاجًا
« wa ra-ayeta nnaasa yadkhoulouna fii diini llaahi afwaajane »
And thou dost see the people enter Allah's Religion in crowds,

فَسَبِّحْ بِحَمْدِ رَبِّكَ وَاسْتَغْفِرْهُ إِنَّهُ كَانَ تَوَّابًا
« fasabbih bismi rabbika wa staghfirhou innahou kaana tawaabane »
Celebrate the praises of thy Lord, and pray for His Forgiveness: For He is Oft-Returning (in Grace and Mercy).

Then, say: :

الله أكبر

« allaahou akbar »

Allah is Great

> الله أكبر
> **Allah is Great**
> « allaahou akbar »

And, do as in the following image:

Then, say three times :

"subhaana rabiyya al-aaddiime » :

سبحان ربي العظيم

Glory be to my God

Then, standing upright again and saying:

"sami-aa llaahou limane hamidah" سمع الله لمن حمده

« Allah listens to those who praise Him »

« rabbanaa walaka lhamd » ربنا و لك الحمد

Praise be to our God

Then, say: :

الله أكبر

« allaahou akbar »

Allah is Great

الله أكبر

Allah is Great

« allaahou akbar »

While prostrating, you have to say three times :

"subhaana rabiyya al-aalaa"

سبحان ربي الأعلى

Glory to my God

Raising the head and saying:

"Allaahou akbar"

الله أكبر

Allah is Great

الله أكبر
Allah is Great
« allaahou akbar »

Then, say a request such as :

اللهم إغفر لي و إرحمني

« Allaahoumma ighfir lii wa rhamenii »

My God, forgive me and have mercy on me

Then slowly bending down to prostrate and saying:

"Allaahou akbar"

الله أكبر

Allah is Great

الله أكبر
Allah is Great
« allaahou akbar »

Once again, while prostrating you have to say 3 times :

"subhaana rabiyya al-aalaa"

سبحان ربي الأعلى

Glory to my God

Raising the head and saying:

"Allaahou akbar"

الله أكبر

Allah is Great

الله أكبر
Allah is Great
« allaahou akbar »

Then, you sit on your knees to recite the tashahhud while moving your finger of your right hand:

التحيات لله و الصلوات و الطيبات،
« attahiyaatou lillaah wa ssalawaatou wa ttayibaate »
All compliments, prayers and pure words are due to Allaah.

السلام عليك أيها النبي ، و رحمة الله و بركاته
«assalaamou aalayeka ayouha nnabii warahmatou llaahi wa barakaatouhou »
Peace be upon you, O Prophet, and the mercy of Allaah and His blessings.

السلام علينا و على عباد الله الصالحين،
« assalaamou aalayenaa wa aalaa aibaadi llahi ssaalihiina »
Peace be upon us and upon the righteous slaves of Allaah.

أشهد أن لا إله إلا الله،
« ashehadou anna laa ilaaha illa llaah »
I bear witness that there is no god except Allaah

و أشهد أن محمدا عبده و رسوله.
«wa ashehadou anna mouhammadane aabedouhou wa rasoulouhou »
and I bear witness that Muhammad is His slave and Messenger

THE THIRD RAKAAH

This is the illustration of the third « RAKAAH »

Then, start your third « RAKAAH» by saying:

الله أكبر

« allaahou akbar »

Allah is Great

- Look at the following image -

الله أكبر
Allah is Great
« allaahou akbar »

Then, recite again silently Al-Fatiha:

بإسم الله الرحمان الرحيم
« bismillaahi rrahmaani rrahiime »
In the name of Allah, Most Gracious, Most Merciful.

الْحَمْدُ لِلَّهِ رَبِّ الْعَالَمِينَ
« alhamdou lilaahi rabbi al-aalamiine »
Praise be to Allah, the Cherisher and Sustainer of the worlds,

الرَّحْمَٰنِ الرَّحِيمِ
« arrahmaani rrahiime »
Most Gracious, Most Merciful,

مَالِكِ يَوْمِ الدِّينِ
« maaliki yawemi ddiine »
Master of the Day of Judgment.

إِيَّاكَ نَعْبُدُ وَإِيَّاكَ نَسْتَعِينُ
« iyyaaka na-aboudo wa iyyaaka nasta-aaiine »
Thee do we worship, and Thine aid we seek.

اهْدِنَا الصِّرَاطَ الْمُسْتَقِيمَ
« ihdina ssiraata almoustaqiime »
Show us the straight way,

»صِرَاطَ الَّذِينَ أَنْعَمْتَ عَلَيْهِمْ غَيْرِ الْمَغْضُوبِ عَلَيْهِمْ وَلَا الضَّالِّينَ. امين.
« siraata lladina ane-aameta aalayehime, ghayri almaghdoubi aalayehime, wala ddaliiine. Amiiiiine »
The way of those on whom Thou hast bestowed Thy Grace, those whose (portion) is not wrath, and who go not astray. Amine.

Then, say: :

الله أكبر

« allaahou akbar »

Allah is Great

> الله أكبر
> **Allah is Great**
> « allaahou akbar »

And, do as in the following image:

Then, say three times :

"subhaana rabiyya al-aaddiime » :

سبحان ربي العظيم

Glory be to my God

Then, standing upright again and saying:

"sami-aa llaahou liman hamidah" سمع الله لمن حمده

« Allah listens to those who praise Him »

« rabbanaa walaka lhamd » ربنا و لك الحمد

Praise be to our God

Then, say:

الله أكبر

« allaahou akbar »

Allah is Great

> الله أكبر
> **Allah is Great**
> « allaahou akbar »

While prostrating, you have to say 3 times :

"subhaana rabiyya al-aalaa"

سبحان ربي الأعلى

Glory to my God

Raising the head and saying:

"Allaahou akbar"

الله أكبر

Allah is Great

الله أكبر
Allah is Great
« allaahou akbar »

Then, say a request such as :

اللهم إغفر لي و إرحمني

« Allaahouma ighfir lii wa rhamnii »

My God, forgive me and have mercy on me

Then slowly bending down to prostrate and saying:

"Allaahou akbar"

الله أكبر

Allah is Great

الله أكبر
Allah is Great
« allaahou akbar »

Once again, while prostrating you have to say 3 times :

"subhaana rabiyya al-aalaa"

سبحان ربي الأعلى

Glory to my God

Then, you sit on your knees to recite the tashahhud and Ibrahimya prayer, while moving your finger of your right hand:
(as written on the following page)

The Tashahhud and Ibrahimya prayer:

التحيات لله و الصلوات و الطيبات،
« attahiyaatou lillaah wa ssalawaatou wa ttayibaate »
All compliments, prayers and pure words are due to Allaah.

السلام عليك أيها النبي ، و رحمة الله و بركاته
«assalaamou aalayeka ayouha nnabii warahmatou llaahi wa barakaatouhou »
Peace be upon you, O Prophet, and the mercy of Allaah and His blessings.

السلام علينا و على عباد الله الصالحين،
« assalaamou aalayenaa wa aalaa aibaadi llaahi ssaalihiina »
Peace be upon us and upon the righteous slaves of Allaah.

أشهد أن لا إله إلا الله،
« ashehadou anna laa ilaaha illa llaah »
I bear witness that there is no god except Allaah

و أشهد أن محمدا عبده و رسوله.
«wa ashehadou anna mouhammadane aabedouhou wa rasoulouhou »
and I bear witness that Muhammad is His slave and Messenger.

اللهم صلي على محمد و على آل محمد
« allahoumma salli aalaa mouhammadine wa aalaa aali mouhammadine »
O Allaah, send prayers upon Muhammad and upon the family of Muhammad,

كما صليت على إبراهيم و على آل إبراهيم
« kamaa sallayeta aalaa ibrahiim wa aalaa aali ibrahiim »
as You sent prayers upon Ibraaheem and the family of Ibraaheem

وبارك على محمد و على آل محمد
« wa baarik aalaa mouhammadine wa aalaa aali mouhammadine »
O Allaah, bless Muhammad and the family of Muhammad

كما باركت على إبراهيم و على آل إبراهيم
« kamaa baarakta aalaa ibrahiim wa aalaa aali ibrahiim »
as You blessed Ibraaheem and the family of Ibraaheem,

في العالمين إنك حميد مجيد.
« fii l aalamiina innaka hamiidoune majiide »
You are indeed Worthy of Praise, Full of Glory.

The termination of the prayers takes place as follows:

The head is turned to the right and you say:

"Assalaamou aalaykoum wa rahmatou llaahi ta-aalaa wa barakaatouh"

السلام عليكم و رحمة الله تعالى و بركاته

Peace, mercy and blessings of Almighty God

Then the head is turned to the left and you say:

"Assalaamou aalaykoum wa rahmatou llaahi ta-aalaa wa barakaatouh"

السلام عليكم و رحمة الله تعالى و بركاته

Peace, mercy and blessings of Almighty God

After finishing your prayer, you can say your request « Dua »

Surah At-Tawba : سورة التوبة

حَسْبِيَ اللَّهُ لَا إِلَهَ إِلَّا هُوَ عَلَيْهِ تَوَكَّلْتُ وَهُوَ رَبُّ الْعَرْشِ الْعَظِيمِ (129)

« hasbiya llaahou, laa ilaaha illa houwa, aalayehi tawakkaltou, wa houwa rabbou l-aarshi l-aadiimi. »

"Allâh is sufficient for me. Lâ ilâha illa Huwa (none has the right to be worshipped but He) in Him I put my trust and He is the Lord of the Mighty Throne. »

HOW TO PRAY
SALAT AL-AISHAA

Number of Rakaahs:
Four Rakaahs.

Recitation of the Quran:
-**Boys**: The first and the second rakaah: recite aloud, the third and the fourth rakaah: recite silently
-**Girls**: Recite silently during all the four Rakaahs.

Time:
Between sunset and midnight.

So, let's start.

بإسم الله الرحمان الرحيم
« bismi llaahi rrahmaani rrahiime »
In the name of Allah, Most Gracious, Most Merciful.

This is the illustration of the first « RAKAAH »

First, stand up, your face towards QIBLA, MECCA

Then, always start with « bismillaah »: in the name of Allah.

You should have the intention to pray and then say:

الله أكبر الله أكبر
«Allaahou akbar, allaahou akbar.»
Allah is Great, Allah is Great

أشهد أن لا إلاه إلا الله
« ashehadou anna laa ilaaha illa llaah »
I bear witness that there is no god but Allah

وأشهد أن محمدا عبده و رسوله
« wa ashehadou anna mohammadane abdouhou wa rassoulouhou »
And I bear witness that Muhammad is His slave and Prophet

حي على الصلاة حي على الفلاح
« hayya alaa ssalaati, hayya halaa lfalaahi »
Come to prayer, come to success

قد قامت الصلاة
«qade qaamati ssalaatou»
Prayer has been established,

الله أكبر الله أكبر
«allaahou akbar , allaahou akbar. »
Allah is Great, Allah is Great

لا إلاه إلا الله
« laa ilaaha illa llaah »
there is no god but Allah.

Then, start your prayer by saying:

الله أكبر

« allaahou akbar »

Allah is Great

- Look at the following image -

> الله أكبر
> **Allah is Great**
> « allaahou akbar »

Then, recite aloud surah Al-Fatiha:

بِإِسْمِ اللهِ الرحمان الرحيم
« bismillaahi rrahmaani rrahiime »
In the name of Allah, Most Gracious, Most Merciful.

الْحَمْدُ لِلَّهِ رَبِّ الْعَالَمِينَ
« alhamdou lillaahi rabbi al-aalamiina »
Praise be to Allah, the Cherisher and Sustainer of the worlds,

الرَّحْمَٰنِ الرَّحِيمِ
« arrahmaani rrahiime »
Most Gracious, Most Merciful,

مَالِكِ يَوْمِ الدِّينِ
« maaliki yawemi ddiine »
Master of the Day of Judgment.

إِيَّاكَ نَعْبُدُ وَإِيَّاكَ نَسْتَعِينُ
« iyyaaka na-aboudo wa iyyaaka nasta-aaiine »
Thee do we worship, and Thine aid we seek.

اهْدِنَا الصِّرَاطَ الْمُسْتَقِيمَ
« ihdina ssiraata almoustaqiime »
Show us the straight way,

»صِرَاطَ الَّذِينَ أَنْعَمْتَ عَلَيْهِمْ غَيْرِ الْمَغْضُوبِ عَلَيْهِمْ وَلَا الضَّالِّينَ. امين.
« siraata lladiina ane-aameta aalayehime, ghayri almaghdoubi aalayehime, wala ddaliine. Amiiiiine »
The way of those on whom Thou hast bestowed Thy Grace, those whose (portion) is not wrath, and who go not astray. Amine.

After finishing ALFATIHA, recite aloud any verse from the Quran: For example: Surah AL IKHLAS

بِاسْمِ اللهِ الرَّحْمٰنِ الرَّحِيْمِ
« bismillaahi rrahmaani rrahiime »
In the Name of Allâh, the Most Beneficent, the Most Merciful.

قُلْ هُوَ اللَّهُ أَحَدٌ
« qoul houa llaahou ahade »
Say "Allâh is (the) One

اللَّهُ الصَّمَدُ
« allaahou ssamade »
The Self-Sufficient Master

لَمْ يَلِدْ وَلَمْ يُولَدْ
« lame yalide walame youlade »
"He begets not, nor was He begotten.

وَلَمْ يَكُنْ لَهُ كُفُوًا أَحَدٌ
« walame yakoune lahou koufou-ane ahade »
And there is none co-equal or comparable unto Him.

Then, say: :

الله أكبر

« allaahou akbar »

Allah is Great

> الله أكبر
> **Allah is Great**
> « allaahou akbar »

And, do as in the following image:

Then, say three times :

"subhaana rabiyya al-aaddiime » :

سبحان ربي العظيم

Glory be to my God

Then, standing upright again and saying:

"sami-aa llaahou liman hamidah" سمع الله لمن حمده

« Allah listens to those who praise Him »

« rabbanaa walaka lhamd » ربنا و لك الحمد

Praise be to our God

Then, say: :

الله أكبر

« allaahou akbar »

Allah is Great

> الله أكبر
> **Allah is Great**
> « allaahou akbar »

While prostrating, you have to say 3 times :

"subhaana rabiyya al-aalaa"

سبحان ربي الأعلى

Glory to my God

Raising the head and saying:

"Allaahou akbar"

الله أكبر

Allah is Great

Then, say a request such as :

اللهم إغفر لي و إرحمني

« Allaahoumaa ighfir lii wa rhamnii »

My God, forgive me and have mercy on me

Then slowly bending down to prostrate and saying:

"Allaahou akbar"

الله أكبر

Allah is Great

Once again, while prostrating you have to say 3 times :

"subhaana rabiyya al-aalaa"

سبحان ربي الأعلى

Glory to my God

THE SECOND « RAKAAH »

This is the illustration of the second « RAKAAH »

Then, stand up again, your face towards the QIBLA, MECCA

Then, start your second RAKAAH by saying:

الله أكبر

« allaahou akbar »

Allah is Great

- **Look at the following image -**

الله أكبر

Allah is Great

« allaahou akbar »

Then, recite once again aloud surah Al-Fatiha:

بِإِسْمِ اللهِ الرحمان الرحيم
« bismillaahi rrahmaani rrahiime »
In the name of Allah, Most Gracious, Most Merciful.

الْحَمْدُ لِلَّهِ رَبِّ الْعَالَمِينَ
« alhamdou lillaahi rabbi al-aalamiine »
Praise be to Allah, the Cherisher and Sustainer of the worlds,

الرَّحْمَٰنِ الرَّحِيمِ
« arrahmaani rrahiime »
Most Gracious, Most Merciful,

مَالِكِ يَوْمِ الدِّينِ
« maaliki yawemi ddiine »
Master of the Day of Judgment.

إِيَّاكَ نَعْبُدُ وَإِيَّاكَ نَسْتَعِينُ
« iyyaaka na-aboudo wa iyyaaka nasta-aaiine »
Thee do we worship, and Thine aid we seek.

اهْدِنَا الصِّرَاطَ الْمُسْتَقِيمَ
« ihdina ssiraata almoustaqiime »
Show us the straight way,

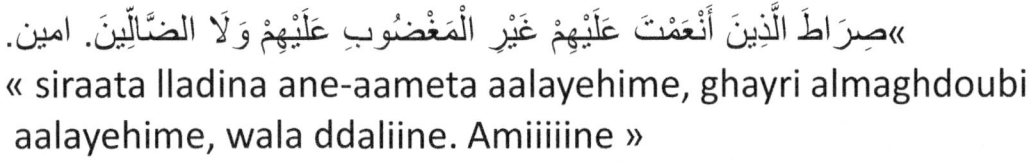

صِرَاطَ الَّذِينَ أَنْعَمْتَ عَلَيْهِمْ غَيْرِ الْمَغْضُوبِ عَلَيْهِمْ وَلَا الضَّالِّينَ. امين.
« siraata lladina ane-aameta aalayehime, ghayri almaghdoubi aalayehime, wala ddaliine. Amiiiiine »
The way of those on whom Thou hast bestowed Thy Grace, those whose (portion) is not wrath, and who go not astray. Amine.

After finishing ALFATIHA, recite aloud any verse from the Quran: For example: سورة النصر *Surah An-Nasr*

بسم الله الرحمن الرحيم
« bismillaahi rrahmaani rrahiime »
In the Name of Allâh, the Most Beneficent, the Most Merciful.

إِذَا جَاءَ نَصْرُ اللَّهِ وَالْفَتْحُ
« idaa jaa a nasrou llaahi walfatehou »
When comes the Help of Allah, and Victory,

وَرَأَيْتَ النَّاسَ يَدْخُلُونَ فِي دِينِ اللَّهِ أَفْوَاجًا
« wa ra-ayeta nnaasa yadkhoulouna fii diini llaahi afwaajane »
And thou dost see the people enter Allah's Religion in crowds,

فَسَبِّحْ بِحَمْدِ رَبِّكَ وَاسْتَغْفِرْهُ إِنَّهُ كَانَ تَوَّابًا
« fasabbih bismi rabbika wa staghfirhou innahou kaana tawaabane »
Celebrate the praises of thy Lord, and pray for His Forgiveness: For He is Oft-Returning (in Grace and Mercy).

Then, say: :

الله أكبر

« allaahou akbar »

Allah is Great

> الله أكبر
> **Allah is Great**
> « allaahou akbar »

And, do as in the following image:

Then, say three times :

"subhaana rabiyya al-aaddiime » :

سبحان ربي العظيم

Glory be to my God

Then, standing upright again and saying:

"sami-aa llaahou limane hamidah" سمع الله لمن حمده

« Allah listens to those who praise Him »

« rabbanaa walaka lhamd » ربنا و لك الحمد

Praise be to our God

Then, say: :

الله أكبر

« allaahou akbar »

Allah is Great

> الله أكبر
> **Allah is Great**
> « allaahou akbar »

While prostrating, you have to say three times :

"subhaana rabiyya al-aalaa"

سبحان ربي الأعلى

Glory to my God

Raising the head and saying:

"Allaahou akbar"

الله أكبر

Allah is Great

الله أكبر
Allah is Great
« allaahou akbar »

Then, say a request such as :

اللهم إغفر لي و إرحمني

« Allaahoumma ighfir lii wa rhamenii »

My God, forgive me and have mercy on me

Then slowly bending down to prostrate and saying:

"Allaahou akbar"

الله أكبر

Allah is Great

الله أكبر
Allah is Great
« allaahou akbar »

Once again, while prostrating you have to say 3 times :

"subhaana rabiyya al-aalaa"

سبحان ربي الأعلى

Glory to my God

Raising the head and saying:

"Allaahou akbar"

الله أكبر

Allah is Great

الله أكبر
Allah is Great
« allaahou akbar »

Then, you sit on your knees to recite the tashahhud while moving your finger of your right hand:

التحيات لله و الصلوات و الطيبات،
« attahiyaatou lillaah wa ssalawaatou wa ttayibaate »
All compliments, prayers and pure words are due to Allaah.

السلام عليك أيها النبي ، و رحمة الله و بركاته
«assalaamou aalayeka ayouha nnabii warahmatou llaahi wa barakaatouhou »
Peace be upon you, O Prophet, and the mercy of Allaah and His blessings.

السلام علينا و على عباد الله الصالحين،
« assalaamou aalayenaa wa aalaa aibaadi llahi ssaalihiina »
Peace be upon us and upon the righteous slaves of Allaah.

أشهد أن لا إله إلا الله،
« ashehadou anna laa ilaaha illa llaah »
I bear witness that there is no god except Allaah

.و أشهد أن محمدا عبده و رسوله
«wa ashehadou anna mouhammadane aabedouhou wa rasoulouhou »
and I bear witness that Muhammad is His slave and Messenger

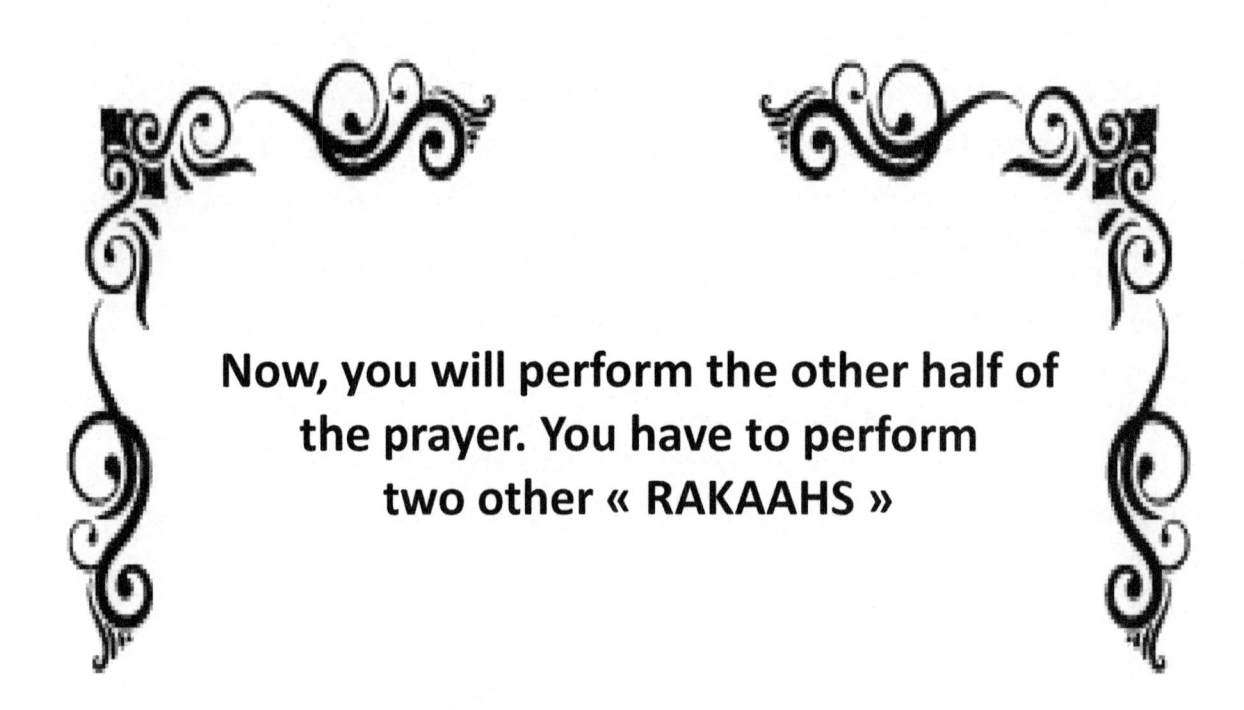

Now, you will perform the other half of the prayer. You have to perform two other « RAKAAHS »

THE THIRD RAKAAH

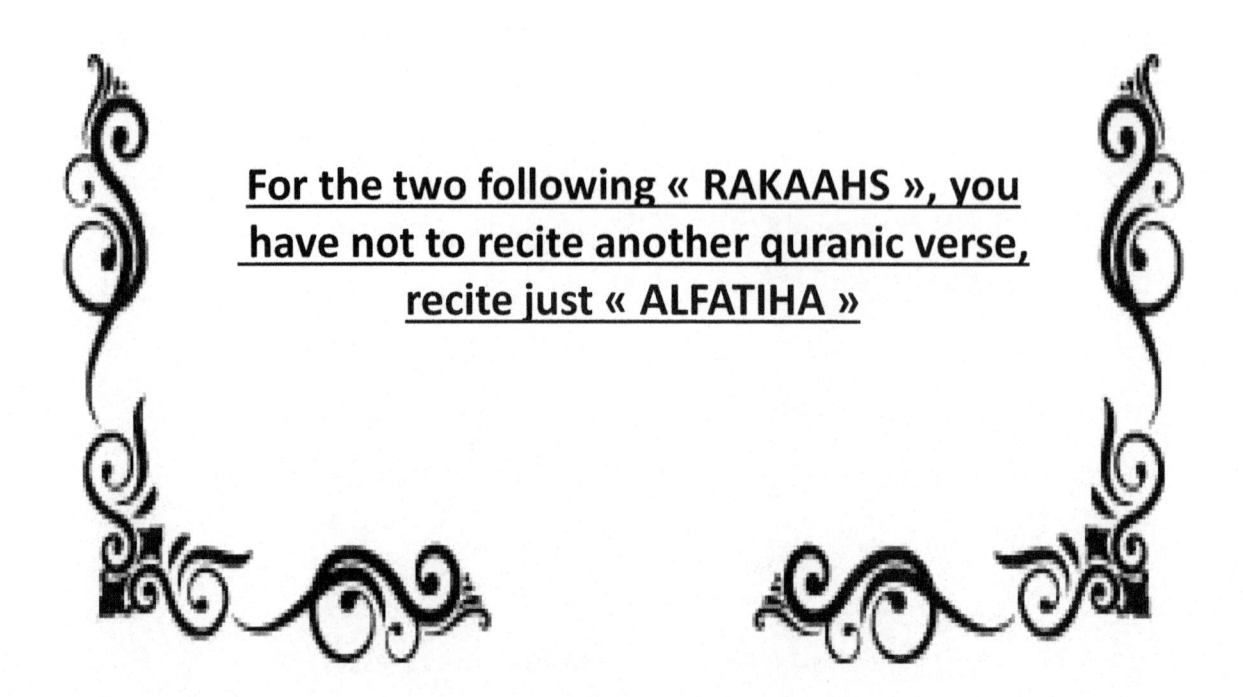

For the two following « RAKAAHS », you have not to recite another quranic verse, recite just « ALFATIHA »

This is the illustration of the third « RAKAAH »

Then, start your third « RAKAAH» by saying:

الله أكبر

« allaahou akbar »

Allah is Great

- Look at the following image -

الله أكبر
Allah is Great
« allaahou akbar »

Then, recite again silently surah Al-Fatiha:

بِاسْمِ اللهِ الرحمان الرحيم
« bismillaahi rrahmaani rrahiime »
In the name of Allah, Most Gracious, Most Merciful.

الْحَمْدُ لِلَّهِ رَبِّ الْعَالَمِينَ
« alhamdou lilaahi rabbi al-aalamiine »
Praise be to Allah, the Cherisher and Sustainer of the worlds,

الرَّحْمَٰنِ الرَّحِيمِ
« arrahmaani rrahiime »
Most Gracious, Most Merciful,

مَالِكِ يَوْمِ الدِّينِ
« maaliki yawemi ddiine »
Master of the Day of Judgment.

إِيَّاكَ نَعْبُدُ وَإِيَّاكَ نَسْتَعِينُ
« iyyaaka na-aboudo wa iyyaaka nasta-aaiine »
Thee do we worship, and Thine aid we seek.

اهْدِنَا الصِّرَاطَ الْمُسْتَقِيمَ
« ihdina ssiraata almoustaqiime »
Show us the straight way,

»صِرَاطَ الَّذِينَ أَنْعَمْتَ عَلَيْهِمْ غَيْرِ الْمَغْضُوبِ عَلَيْهِمْ وَلَا الضَّالِّينَ. امين.
« siraata lladina ane-aameta aalayehime, ghayri almaghdoubi aalayehime, wala ddaliine. Amiiiiine »
The way of those on whom Thou hast bestowed Thy Grace, those whose (portion) is not wrath, and who go not astray. Amine.

Then, say: :

الله أكبر

« allaahou akbar »

Allah is Great

> الله أكبر
> **Allah is Great**
> « allaahou akbar »

And, do as in the following image:

Then, say three times :

"subhaana rabiyya al-aaddiime » :

سبحان ربي العظيم

Glory be to my God

Then, standing upright again and saying:

"sami-aa llaahou liman hamidah" سمع الله لمن حمده

« Allah listens to those who praise Him »

« rabbanaa walaka lhamd » ربنا و لك الحمد

Praise be to our God

Then, say:

الله أكبر

« allaahou akbar »

Allah is Great

الله أكبر
Allah is Great
« allaahou akbar »

While prostrating, you have to say 3 times :

"subhaana rabiyya al-aalaa"

سبحان ربي الأعلى

Glory to my God

Raising the head and saying:

"Allaahou akbar"

الله أكبر

Allah is Great

الله أكبر
Allah is Great
« allaahou akbar »

Then, say a request such as :

اللهم إغفر لي و إرحمني

« Allaahouma ighfir lii wa rhamnii »

My God, forgive me and have mercy on me

Then slowly bending down to prostrate and saying:

"Allaahou akbar"

الله أكبر

Allah is Great

الله أكبر
Allah is Great
« allaahou akbar »

Once again, while prostrating you have to say 3 times :

"subhaana rabiyya al-aalaa"

سبحان ربي الأعلى

Glory to my God

FOURTH RAKAAH

This is the illustration of the fourth « RAKAAH »

Then, start your fourth « RAKAAH» by saying:

الله أكبر

« allaahou akbar »

Allah is Great

- Look at the following image -

الله أكبر
Allah is Great
« allaahou akbar »

Then, recite once again silently surah Al-Fatiha:

بإسم الله الرحمان الرحيم
« bismillaahi rrahmaani rrahiime »
In the name of Allah, Most Gracious, Most Merciful.

الْحَمْدُ لِلَّهِ رَبِّ الْعَالَمِينَ
« alhamdou lilaahi rabbi al-aalamiine »
Praise be to Allah, the Cherisher and Sustainer of the worlds,

الرَّحْمَٰنِ الرَّحِيمِ
« arrahmaani rrahiime »
Most Gracious, Most Merciful,

مَالِكِ يَوْمِ الدِّينِ
« maaliki yawemi ddiine »
Master of the Day of Judgment.

إِيَّاكَ نَعْبُدُ وَإِيَّاكَ نَسْتَعِينُ
« iyyaaka na-aboudo wa iyyaaka nasta-aaiine »
Thee do we worship, and Thine aid we seek.

اهْدِنَا الصِّرَاطَ الْمُسْتَقِيمَ
« ihdinaa ssiraata almoustaqiime »
Show us the straight way,

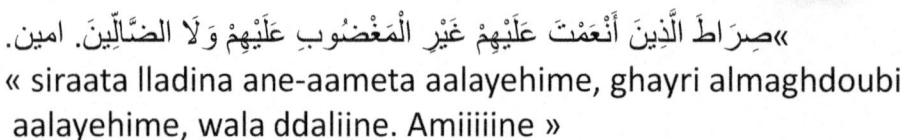

»صِرَاطَ الَّذِينَ أَنْعَمْتَ عَلَيْهِمْ غَيْرِ الْمَغْضُوبِ عَلَيْهِمْ وَلَا الضَّالِّينَ. امين.
« siraata lladina ane-aameta aalayehime, ghayri almaghdoubi aalayehime, wala ddaliine. Amiiiiine »
The way of those on whom Thou hast bestowed Thy Grace, those whose (portion) is not wrath, and who go not astray. Amine.

Then, say: :

الله أكبر

« allaahou akbar »

Allah is Great

> الله أكبر
> **Allah is Great**
> « allaahou akbar »

And, do as in the following image:

Then, say three times :

"subhaana rabiyya al-aaddiime » :

سبحان ربي العظيم

Glory be to my God

Then, standing upright again and saying:

"sami-aa llaahou limane hamidah" سمع الله لمن حمده

« Allah listens to those who praise Him »

« rabbanaa walaka lhamd » ربنا و لك الحمد

Praise be to our God

Then, say: :

الله أكبر

« allaahou akbar »

Allah is Great

الله أكبر
Allah is Great
« allaahou akbar »

While prostrating, you have to say 3 times :

"subhaana rabiyya al-aalaa"

سبحان ربي الأعلى

Glory to my God

Raising the head and saying:

"Allaahou akbar"

الله أكبر

Allah is Great

الله أكبر
Allah is Great
« allaahou akbar »

Then, say a request such as :

اللهم إغفر لي و إرحمني

« Allaahouma ighfir lii wa rhamnii »

My God, forgive me and have mercy on me

Then slowly bending down to prostrate and saying:

"Allaahou akbar"

الله أكبر

Allah is Great

الله أكبر
Allah is Great
« allaahou akbar »

Once again, while prostrating you have to say 3 times :

"subhaana rabiyya al-aalaa"

سبحان ربي الأعلى

Glory to my God

Raising the head and saying:

"Allaahou akbar"

الله أكبر

Allah is Great

الله أكبر
Allah is Great
« allaahou akbar »

Then, you sit on your knees to recite the tashahhud and Ibrahimya prayer, while moving your finger of your right hand:
(as written on the following page)

The Tashahhud and Ibrahimya prayer:

التحيات لله و الصلوات و الطيبات،
« attahiyaatou lillaah wa ssalawaatou wa ttayibaate »
All compliments, prayers and pure words are due to Allaah.

السلام عليك أيها النبي ، و رحمة الله و بركاته
« assalaamou aalayeka ayouha nnabii warahmatou llaahi wa barakaatouhou »
Peace be upon you, O Prophet, and the mercy of Allaah and His blessings.

السلام علينا و على عباد الله الصالحين،
« assalaamou aalayenaa wa aalaa aibaadi llaahi ssaalihiina »
Peace be upon us and upon the righteous slaves of Allaah.

أشهد أن لا إله إلا الله،
« ashehadou anna laa ilaaha illa llaah »
I bear witness that there is no god except Allaah

و أشهد أن محمدا عبده و رسوله.
« wa ashehadou anna mouhammadane aabedouhou wa rasoulouhou »
and I bear witness that Muhammad is His slave and Messenger.

اللهم صلي على محمد و على آل محمد
« allahoumma salli aalaa mouhammadine wa aalaa aali mouhammadine »
O Allaah, send prayers upon Muhammad and upon the family of Muhammad,

كما صليت على إبراهيم و على آل إبراهيم
« kamaa sallayeta aalaa ibrahiim wa aalaa aali ibrahiim »
as You sent prayers upon Ibraaheem and the family of Ibraaheem,

وبارك على محمد و على آل محمد
« wa baarik aalaa mouhammadine wa aalaa aali mouhammadine »
O Allaah, bless Muhammad and the family of Muhammad

كما باركت على إبراهيم و على آل إبراهيم
« kamaa baarakta aalaa ibrahiim wa aalaa aali ibrahiim »
as You blessed Ibraaheem and the family of Ibraaheem,

في العالمين إنك حميد مجيد.
« fii l aalamiina innaka hamiidoune majiide »
You are indeed Worthy of Praise, Full of Glory.

The termination of the prayers takes place as follows:

The head is turned to the right and you say:

"Assalaamou aalaykoum wa rahmatou llaahi ta-aalaa wa barakaatouh"

السلام عليكم و رحمة الله تعالى و بركاته

Peace, mercy and blessings of Almighty God

Then the head is turned to the left and you say:

"Assalaamou aalaykoum wa rahmatou llaahi ta-aalaa wa barakaatouh"

السلام عليكم و رحمة الله تعالى و بركاته

Peace, mercy and blessings of Almighty God

After finishing your prayer, you can say your request « Dua »

Sura Ad-Dukhaan (Ayaa 12) : سورة الدخان

رَبَّنَا اكْشِفْ عَنَّا الْعَذَابَ إِنَّا مُؤْمِنُونَ

« rabbanaa k-shif aannaa l-aadaaba innaa mou-minouna. »

"Our Lord. Remove the torment from us, really we shall become believers."

The five daily prayers recapitulation

Prayers	Rakkahs	Composition of each prayer	TIME OF PRAYERS
Al-Fajr	2	Two loudly Rakaahs + Tashahhud + Ibrahimya Prayer + Salam Aalyekoume	Dawn, before sunrise
Adduher	4	Two silent Rakaahs + Tashahhud + Two silent Rakaahs + Tashahhud + Ibrahimya Prayer + Salam Aalyekoume	midday, after the sun passes its highest
Al-Aaser	4	Two silent Rakaahs + Tashahhud + Two silent Rakaahs + Tashahhud + Ibrahimya Prayer + Salam Aalyekoume	The late part of the afternoon
Al-Maghreb	3	Two loudly Rakaahs + Tashahhud + One silent Rakkah + Tashahhud + Ibrahimya Prayer + Salam Aalyekoume	Just after sunset
Al-Aishaa	4	Two loudly Rakaahs + Tashahhud + Two silent Rakaahs + Tashahhud + Ibrahimya Prayer + Salam Aalyekoume	Between sunset and midnight

Once again, it's very important to mention that **girls** have to recite Quran **silently** during all their prayers.

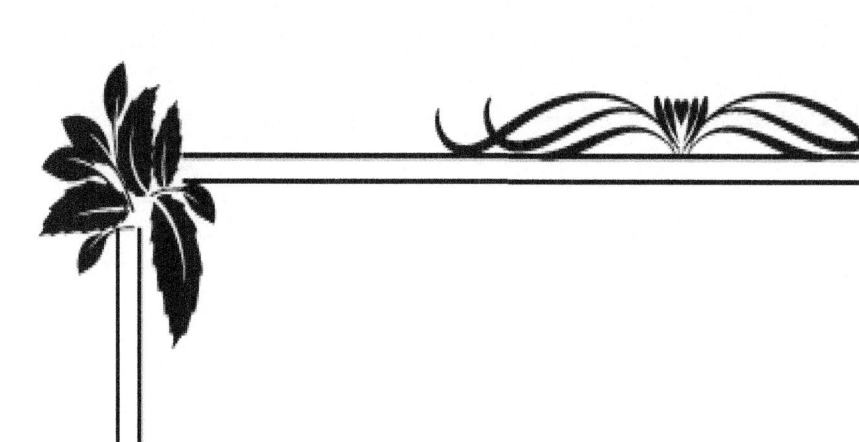

ABLUTION in Islam

Of course, if you want to pray, you should keep yourself in state of clean and pure. And so as to be so, you have to perform ablution.
"Prayer without ablution is invalid »

Indeed, ablution « ALWOUDOU » is an islamic procedure for cleansing the whole body or parts of it. The ablution is normally done in preparation for formal daily five obligatory prayers or before handling and reading the Quran.

There are three types of ablution:

1/ Partial ablution: washing parts of the body using water. This type of ablution is an acte for purifying some activities such as urination, defecation, flatulence, deep sleep, light bleeding. This ablution is perfomed everyday.

2/ Dry ablution: « Attayamoume »: replacing water with stone or sand when there is no water.

3/ Full ablution: washing the whole body using water after sexual intercourse, childbirth or menstruation. This involves similar steps to the above (1rst ablution), with the addition of rinsing the left and right sides of the body as well.

In this part of this book, we will present for you how you can perfom islamic partial ablution step by step so as to practice your daily prayers correctly.

So, when someone determines to cleanse oneself for prayer, for the sake of Allah. Then, one begins with :

بإسم الله الرحمان الرحيم
« bismi llaahi rrahmaani rrahiime »
In the name of Allah, Most Gracious, Most Merciful.

And with water, one then begins to wash some parts of one's body as follows:

بإسم الله الرحمان الرحيم

« bismi llaahi rrahmaani rrahiime »
In the name of Allah, Most Gracious, Most Merciful.

1/ Wash the hands three times, making sure that the water reaches between the fingers and all over the hands up to the wrist

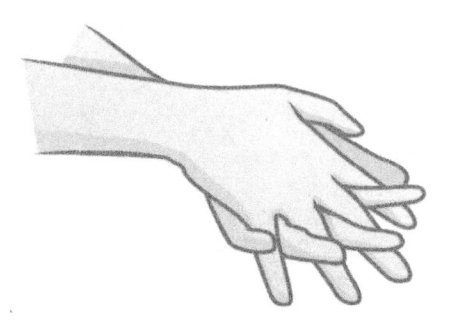

2/ Wash the mouth three times, bringing a handful of water to the mouth and rinsing thoroughly.

3/ Wash the nose three times, using the right hand to bring water up to the nose, sniffing the water, and using the left hand to expel it.

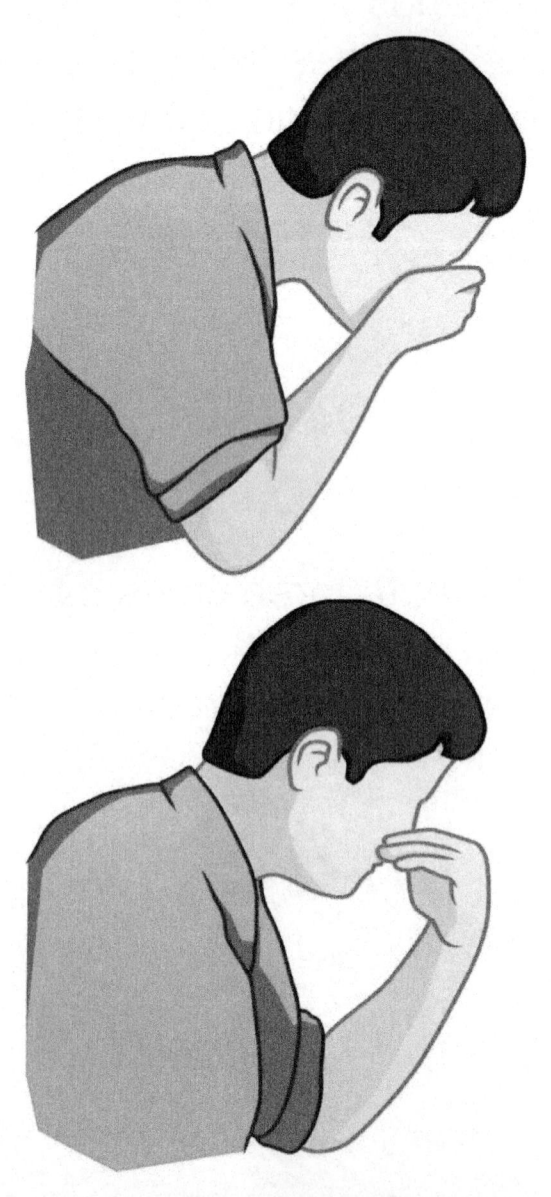

4/ Wash the face three times, from the forehead to the chin and from ear to ear.

5/ Wash the arms three times, up to the elbows, starting with the right arm.

First, the right arm.

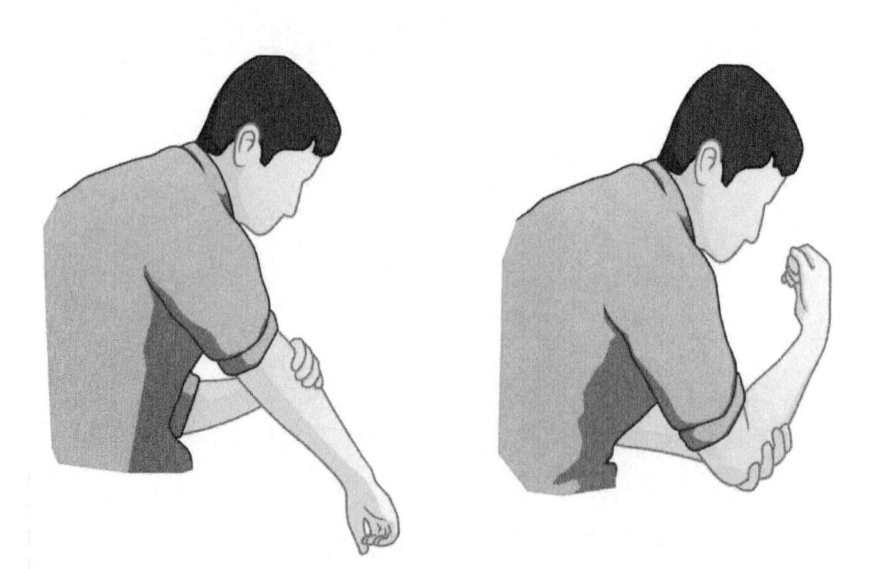

Then, the left arm.

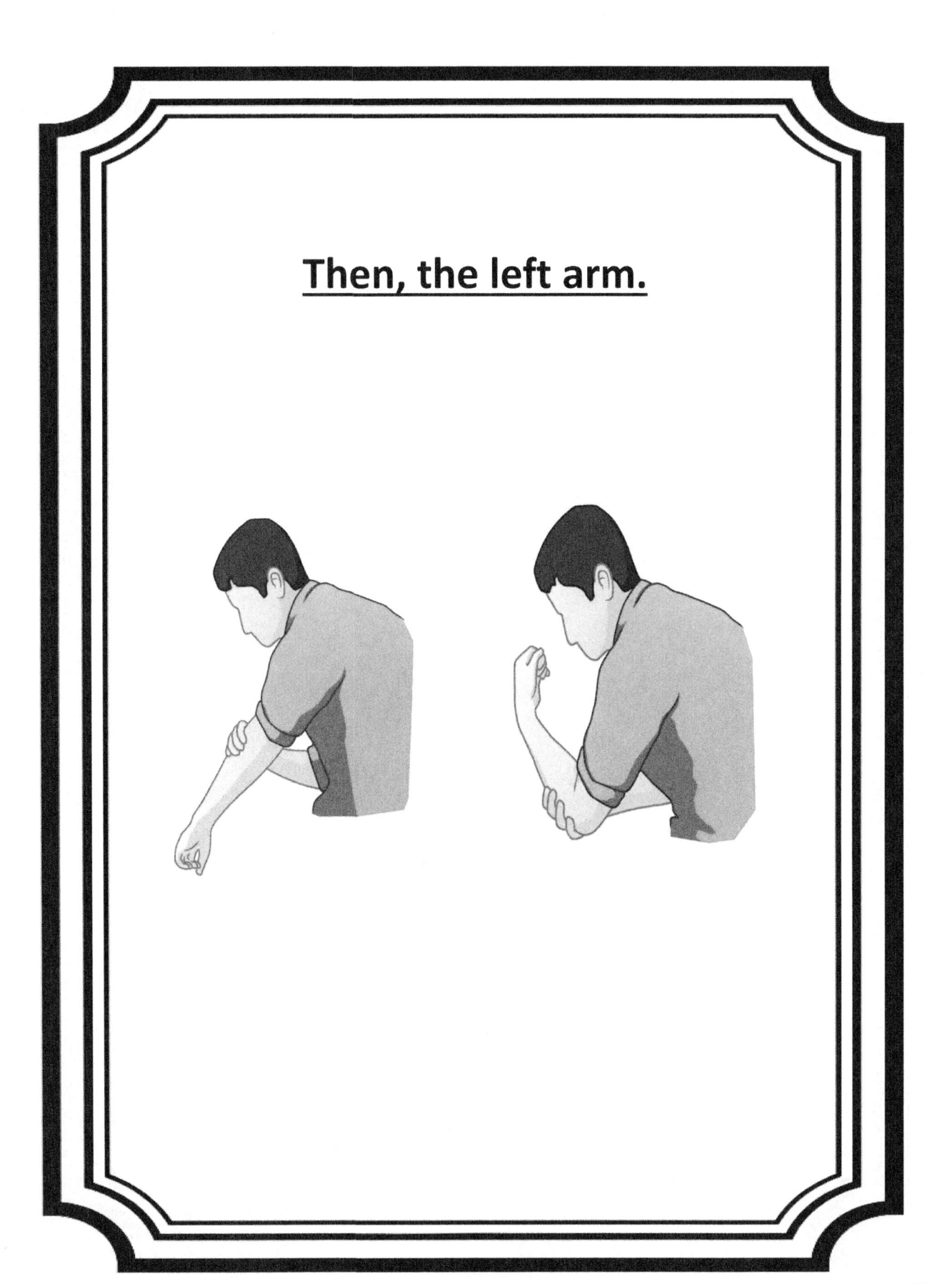

6/ Wash the head one time, using wet Hands to wipe over the head from front to back and front again.

7/ Wash the ears one time, using wet fingers to wipe the inside and outside of the ears.

8/ Wash the feet three times, up to the ankles, starting with the right.

So, first the right foot.

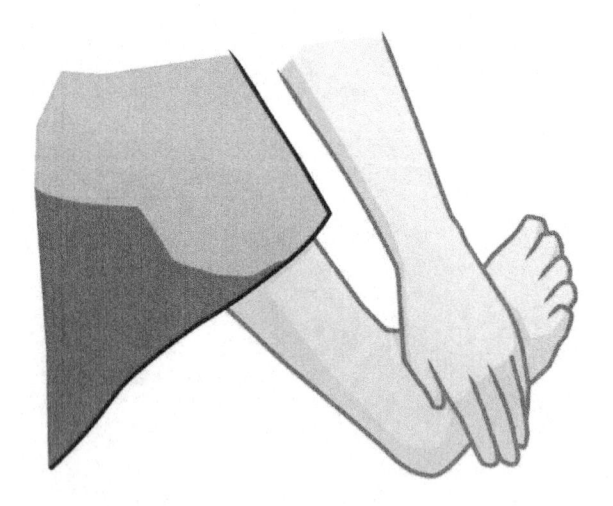

Then, wash the left foot.

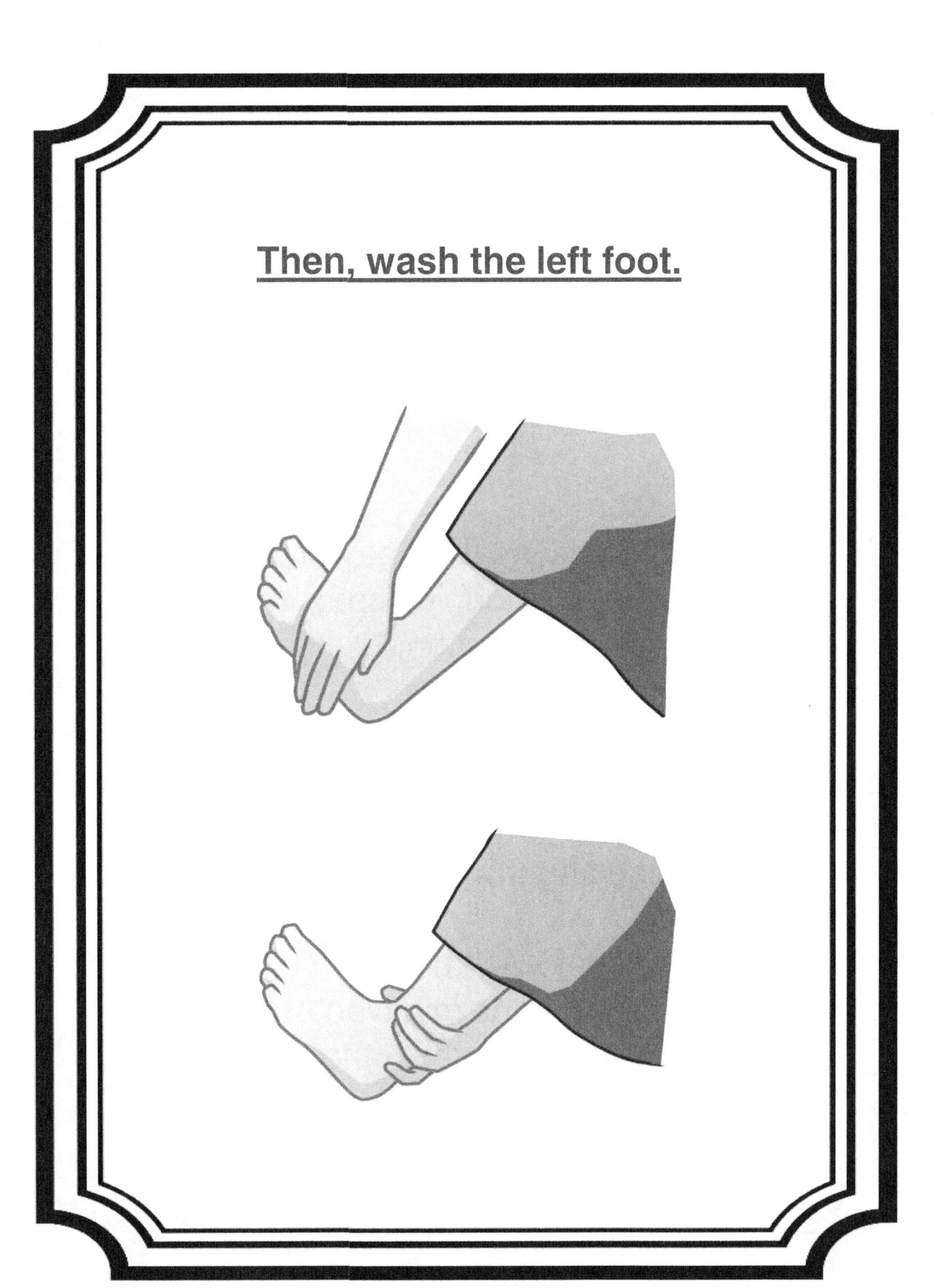

It's very important to mention that
before each everyday prayer,
the muslim person does not need
to repeat the ablution « al woudou »
if it is not broken.

* * * * *

And the actions that may break
the ablution include:
- Urination,
- Defecation,
- Flatulence,
- Deep sleep,
Falling unconscious,
Bleeding from a wound.

Of course after each urination or each
defecation, the parts involved are to be
washed before performing the ablution..

COPY RIGHTS RESERVED 2020
TAMOH ART PUBLISHING

Printed in Great Britain
by Amazon